26 in 26
Neighborhood Resource Centers
26 Neighborhood Strategies in a 26 month time frame
A Grant Funded by the LSTA
(Library Services & Technology Act)

CITY OF
RIVERSIDE

Riverside Public Library

STARTUP
COMMUNITIES

STARTUP

COMMUNITIES

BUILDING AN ENTREPRENEURIAL ECOSYSTEM IN YOUR CITY

BRAD FELD

WILEY

John Wiley & Sons, Inc.

Library of Congress Cataloging-in-Publication Data:

Feld, Brad.
    Startup communities : building an entrepreneurial ecosystem in your city / Brad Feld.
       pages cm
    Includes index.
    ISBN 978-1-118-44154-1 (cloth); 978-1-118-48333-6 (ebk); 978-1-118-48330-5 (ebk);
    978-1-118-48331-2 (ebk)
       1. Entrepreneurship. 2. New business enterprises—Environmental aspects. 3. Communities—Social aspects. I. Title.
    HB615.F45 2012
    658.1'1—dc23

                                                                        2012028586

Printed in the United States of America.

10 9 8 7 6 5 4 3

To Len Fassler, who has taught me more about entrepreneurship than anyone else on this planet.

CONTENTS

CONTENTS

FOREWORD

During the past three decades, startups in the United States have created nearly 40 million American jobs, all the net job creation in the country over that period. As we recover from a deep recession, our ability to innovate, build iconic companies, put people back to work, and inspire the world will once again be determined by whether entrepreneurs continue taking chances on a dream to start a business. After all, the story of America has always been the story of entrepreneurs going against the grain to imagine a better tomorrow.

On January 31, 2010, President Obama announced the creation of the Startup America initiative, telling the American people, "Entrepreneurs embody the promise of America: the idea that if you have a good idea and are willing to work hard and see it through, you can succeed in this country. And in fulfilling this promise, entrepreneurs also play a critical role in expanding our economy and creating jobs."

On that same day we launched the Startup America Partnership, the privately funded component of the Startup America initiative, based on a simple premise: the leading source of job creation in this country comes from young companies starting up, growing, and innovating. One of our goals through the Startup America Partnership is to support regional startup ecosystems throughout the country where entrepreneurs, investors, local leaders, universities, and other partners foster an environment ripe for startup activity.

Brad Feld has been a pioneer in developing regional ecosystems, first with TechStars, and more recently as one of the leaders on the Startup Colorado regional initiative. He has taken what he has learned and created this book to help shape the thinking about best practices for developing startup communities.

At America Online (AOL), Zipcar, and LivingSocial, I've experienced firsthand the significant contribution that a strong entrepreneurial ecosystem has to a business. While Silicon Valley is the iconic example, we are seeing success and potential in other places as well, like Washington, D.C.; Chicago; Denver; Boston; Seattle; Portland; Austin; Raleigh; and Nashville.

But the startup revolution isn't limited to these cities—any locality in the United States can build a vibrant startup community if it strategically brings together the key partners who support growth. In fact, the barriers to entry have never been lower for many sectors across the economy. That's why we launched the Startup America initiative, and that's why this book is such an important contribution: Brad does a great job using the Boulder, Colorado, regional ecosystem as a blueprint for creating and developing a sustainable startup community in any city. If you want to know how to usher in a new wave of job creation, innovation, and growth in your city, I recommend reading this book.

As we emerge from a difficult period in our economic history, we once again turn to entrepreneurs to lead the way to a brighter tomorrow. These startups, the brave men and women behind them, and the many mentors who complement their efforts form the backbone of the startup ecosystem. Brad's book will help you understand how that process works, and will provide you with the tools you need to achieve results anywhere in the United States.

Come join us on this startup revolution.

STEVE CASE
Chairman, Startup America Partnership
Chairman and CEO, Revolution LLC
August 2012

PREFACE

n the fall of 2008 the world financial markets were rocked in an unprecedented way. The global financial crisis that ensued created massive uncertainty across our society and resulted in extraordinary actions by governments and companies throughout the world.

In a parallel universe, something else was happening. Entrepreneurial companies such as Facebook, Twitter, LinkedIn, and Zynga were growing at an equally unprecedented rate. While these companies, and many others, were emerging from Silicon Valley, communities across the country were brimming with startup activity. My hometown of Boulder had become known throughout the world as a great startup community, but cities like New York, Boston, Seattle, Portland, Chicago, and Austin were also seen as nexuses of startup activity.

As the macroeconomic impact of the financial crisis was felt throughout 2009 and 2010 and society tried to readjust to the new economic reality and constraints generated by the collapse of many traditional and well-established institutions, the startups kept being born, growing, and adding jobs.

In early 2011 the world started to notice. On January 31, President Obama acknowledged the importance of entrepreneurship to our global economy through the launch of Startup America. He stated:

> Entrepreneurs embody the promise of America: the idea that if you have a good idea and are willing to work hard and see it through, you can succeed in this country. And in fulfilling this promise, entrepreneurs also play a critical role in expanding our economy and creating jobs.
>
> —*President Barack Obama, @BarackObama*

Suddenly entrepreneurship was at the forefront of the discussion. While entrepreneurs continued to toil away building their companies from scratch, it became clear that entrepreneurship was a global theme—one that impacted every geography, industry, market, and demographic throughout the world. Overnight everyone started talking about entrepreneurship as the way to revitalize our global economy.

No longer was entrepreneurship limited to a small set of risk takers located in a few specific cities. State and local government became interested. Universities dusted off their entrepreneurship initiatives. Angel groups visibly reemerged, VCs became popular again, and large companies created new startup programs.

All this activity has created an enormous amount of noise that runs the risk of drowning out the powerful signal that is entrepreneurship. It won't matter in the long run, as entrepreneurs are going to do what they do, which is create new things (products, companies, jobs, and industries) out of nothing, but it occurred to me that there were powerful lessons that we could learn from the experience I've had in Boulder over the past 16 years.

From this came the Boulder Thesis, a new framework for creating and building a startup community in your city. I have a deeply held belief that you can create a long-term, vibrant, sustainable startup community in any city in the world, but it's hard and takes the right kind of philosophy, approach, leadership, and dedication over a long period of time. Hence, this book, whose goal is to help you understand how to do this and give you the tools to create an amazing startup community in your city.

AUDIENCE

This book is aimed at anyone who wants to be involved in creating, building, and sustaining a startup community in their city. Because entrepreneurs are at the heart of every startup and every startup community, this book is for every entrepreneur.

Startup communities consist of many more participants than just entrepreneurs. Government, universities, investors, mentors, service providers, and large companies play key roles in the development of a startup community. This book is for anyone in those organizations interested in entrepreneurs and startup communities.

Startups have employees who are critical participants in the startup community. Some of these employees will go on to be entrepreneurs and start their own companies; others will work for a range of startups over their careers. They, too, can benefit from many of the ideas in this book.

There are many people studying entrepreneurship, economic development, and innovation, both in government and university settings. Whether you are doing research, creating policy, or just trying to understand what is going on, this book is for you.

Recently, the media has once again become infatuated with entrepreneurship. Unlike the late 1990s when there was relatively little critical thinking in the mix, this time around many journalists and writers are trying to really understand what is going on below the pretty, glossy surface of rich, famous, and successful entrepreneurs. I hope this book will help.

I've been talking about the ideas of a startup community for a number of years and have lived them as an entrepreneur, one of the leaders of the Boulder startup community, and a participant in many other startup communities. By codifying my thoughts and ideas in this book, it forced me to think deeply about them. I hope you benefit from this effort as you explore your own startup community.

OVERVIEW OF THE CONTENTS

After a brief introduction, I'll spend some time exploring the Boulder startup community. I'll go through a brief history, dating back to the 1970s, and include several perspectives besides my own.

I'll then go deep into the principles of a vibrant startup community. I will explore several historical frameworks, describe the Boulder Thesis, and explain the various components of it.

I'll then explore the different participants in a startup community. I separate the participants into two categories—leaders and feeders—and I'll describe in depth both the characteristics of each as well as what they can do to help, as well as hinder, the startup community.

Given an understanding of the participants, I'll discuss the attributes of leadership in a startup community. I'll follow this with a thorough exploration of a set of classical problems that startup communities encounter.

I'll then give a bunch of examples of activities and events that drive the startup community. Many of these examples will come from the people in the Boulder startup community who actually created the activities in the first place. My hope is that these examples will help create a better understanding of the leadership dynamics around startup communities. I'll wrap this up with a detailed look at the power of accelerators to a startup community, using our experience with TechStars as an example.

I'll shift gears and explore the involvement of the university in a startup community. Again I'll use a set of examples from Boulder to help create a better understanding of what's actually going on and how a university can participate effectively. We'll then spend some time on the contrast between entrepreneurs and government and how this often plays out in the development of a startup community.

Near the end of the book, I'll describe a set of clear approaches that generate real power throughout the startup community over a long period of time. I'll use some of Boulder's weaknesses to explore how a successful startup community can continue to improve and grow. Finally, with the help of Paul Kedrosky of the Kauffman Foundation, I'll explore some common myths about startup communities.

I'll finish with a few examples of how to get started, from Iceland, Omaha, and the Startup America Partnership, leaving you with the belief that you can create a vibrant startup community anywhere in the world.

ADDITIONAL MATERIALS

Startup Communities is the first of several books in the Startup Revolution series. The Startup Revolution website (http://startuprev.com) has links to numerous additional resources, including the Startup Communities website (http://communities.startuprev.com). This site includes a blog that we regularly update with stories about startup communities around the world, a discussion board for those interested in startup communities, events that I'll be participating in around startup communities, and resources for anyone interested in creating a startup community.

ACKNOWLEDGMENTS

Because this is my fourth book, I theoretically knew what I was getting into when I started writing it. However, as with each of my other books, there came a time during the process when I was overwhelmed by the amount of work I had in front of me. Each time, my amazing wife, Amy Batchelor, has been there to help out, keep me company, whisper sweet nothings in my ear, and be a calming and supporting influence.

Many people have helped me develop the Boulder Thesis, both through action and long discussions about what is needed and what is going on in Boulder. My partners at Foundry Group, Jason Mendelson, Ryan McIntyre, and Seth Levine top the list, along with David Cohen, the co-founder and CEO of TechStars. I've learned an amazing amount from working alongside you guys.

As I started working on this book, I got early and regular feedback from Jason Mendelson, Amy Batchelor, David Cohen, Brad Bernthal, Phil Weiser, Paul Kedrosky, and Yoav Lurie. You will see your fingerprints throughout the book.

A special note of thanks goes to Brad Bernthal. When I was first sketching out the idea for the book, we had a long conversation about what turned into the Boulder Thesis. I asked him to write a foreword for the book well before I had written much. As I got deep into writing, I realized that his foreword was an excellent draft for Chapter 3: Principles of a Vibrant Startup Community. Brad graciously permitted me to repurpose his foreword for this chapter.

There are a number of contributions throughout this book from other leaders of startup communities, many, but not all, from Boulder. Each responded quickly, when asked, to a request for 500–1,000 words on a specific topic I assigned them. I've incorporated their contributions in the book and thank them in the order in which they appear: Kyle Lefkoff, Mark Solon, David Cohen, Tim Enwall, Robert Reich, Jason Mendelson, Marc Nager, Ef Rodriguez, Tim Falls, Tom Markiewicz, Brad Bernthal, Andrew Hyde, Ryan Martens, David Tisch, Bill Aulet, Phil Weiser, Ben Limmer, Bart Lorang, Christian Renaud, Seth Levine, Bruce Wyman, Lucy Sanders, Paul Kedrosky, John Ives, Bala Kamallakharan, Jeff Slobotski, Scott Case, and Donna Harris.

My assistant, Kelly Collins, continues to be an invaluable part of my work life. Whenever I tell her "I'm vanishing for a while—keep everyone away from me" she merely smiles, knowing I'll still be available all the time, but nevertheless magically makes the volume of external stimuli decrease. Thanks for that and for everything else you do for me.

Our director of IT, Ross Carlson, helped put together the Startup Revolution website (http://startuprev.com) and continues to make sure all the tech runs smoothly.

The Kauffman Foundation, which I first encountered through my work with Jana Matthews in the mid-1990s, has been a superb resource for me, as well as many other entrepreneurs throughout the United States. I'm especially grateful to Paul Kedrosky and Lesa Mitchell for all of the time they spend with me.

The team that I work with at Wiley, especially Bill Falloon, Meg Freeborn, and Tiffany Charbonier, have been awesome.

Finally, there are thousands of entrepreneurs I have worked with and many more people who I have encountered along the way as I spread the message of entrepreneurship and startup communities wherever I go. Y'all are doing the real work. Thanks for the opportunity to know you, work with you, and learn from you.

CHAPTER ONE

INTRODUCTION

Startups are at the core of everything we do. An individual's life is a startup that begins at birth. Every city was once a startup, as was every company, every institution, and every project. As humans, we are wired to start things.

Today, we are in the midst of a massive shift from the hierarchical society that has dominated the industrial era to a networked society that has been emergent throughout the information era. The Internet is ushering in a postinformation era, one in which the machines have already taken over and are waiting patiently for us to catch up with them. This postinformation era is one in which man and machine are interwoven.

In this world, the network dominates in both the online and the physical world. Throughout the network are nodes, each of which began as a startup. Nodes are continually emerging, and a rigid, top-down hierarchy no longer dominates. The energy, activity, and innovation in society is diffused across the network and concentrated in unexpected places that often didn't exist before.

In the physical world, much of this energy, activity, and innovation occur in small geographic regions, which I call "startup communities." Academics call them "clusters," and there are several theories about how they were created, what caused them to grow and evolve, and what happened as they matured.

These startup communities are appearing everywhere. They are no longer limited to historically well-known entrepreneurial regions and large cities such as Silicon Valley, Boston, New York, and Seattle. Startup communities in cities around the United States, both large and small, such as Boulder; Los Angeles; Chicago; Washington, DC; Portland; and Austin are seeing incredible activity and growth. Although many of these cities have a history of entrepreneurial activity, their growth, development, and importance in this economic cycle is unique.

The way startup communities are created and evolve has changed profoundly as a result of our networked society. It is critically important to understand this shift as it relates to economics and innovation because it's not slowing down anytime soon.

In this book, I'll discuss a new approach to building a startup community, which I call the Boulder Thesis. I strongly believe that startup communities can be built in any city and the future economic progress of cities, regions, countries, and society at large is dependent on creating, building, and sustaining startup communities over a long period of time. This book will show you how, both in theory and in practice.

THE EXAMPLE OF BOULDER

Through this book, I use the Boulder startup community as an example. Since I've only lived here since 1995, this is not intended to be a comprehensive history of the Boulder startup community. I don't mean any disrespect to all of the other people who have helped make the Boulder startup community amazing, or who were involved before I moved to town. However, by not trying to create a history, I can cover enough ground to give you a feeling for how things evolved, while I focus on the underlying principles that you can apply to building your startup community.

As I'll discuss in a later chapter, Boulder actually has five startup communities: tech (software/Internet), biotech, clean tech, natural foods, and lifestyles of health and sustainability (LOHAS). These five startup communities exist in parallel universes. My time and expertise have been focused on the tech segment. I periodically have intersection points with the other startup communities through friends, events, and an occasional personal investment in a company outside of tech, but my understanding, experience, and engagement with these other segments are limited.

Throughout this book I've asked others to give their perspective on the key events and activities around the startup community. It will be clear whenever the example is in someone else's voice. I've also brought in several examples from other startup communities when there were activities in Boulder that touched them in a meaningful way, such as TechStars.

My hope is that you do not view the use of Boulder here as "Boulder tooting its own horn." I use Boulder as an example of a lasting and vibrant startup community because I know it extremely well (at least one segment). This approach is called synecdoche, where the part stands for the whole. There are many things the Boulder startup community can do better and many more for it to discover as we continue on our journey; my hope is that by exploring it in depth it helps you with your journey in your startup community.

HOW THIS BOOK WORKS

I'll start with some storytelling, and then I'll get to the principles of a sustainable startup community. I'll break it down into small pieces and I'll give you a full set of tools to work with. I'll try to keep it light along the way with plenty of examples. Although this book is not a textbook, nor is it an academic treatise laden with footnotes and references, it is a serious book. My goal is to give you a framework and tools to create and enhance a startup community in your city.

CHAPTER TWO

THE BOULDER STARTUP COMMUNITY

n November 1995, I left Boston and moved to Boulder. I'd gone to college at MIT and had lived in Boston for 12 years. However, Boston wasn't my home; I'd grown up in Dallas and my wife, Amy, had grown up in Alaska. When I sold my first company at age 28, I promised Amy that we'd leave Boston by the time I was 30. Two months before I turned 30, Amy told me she was moving to Boulder and I was welcome to join her if I wanted to.

We'd both been to Boulder and loved Colorado. Neither of us wanted to live in the Bay Area, which was a logical choice given the work I do, but we wanted either ocean or mountains wherever we lived. Because we were both attracted to the western United States and the Rocky Mountains, we figured we'd give Boulder a try and if it didn't work out, we'd just keep heading west.

After six months, we loved Boulder and never looked back. When we moved here, we knew only one person, and he and his wife moved away a few months later. However, within a year we had already found a community of friends and entrepreneurs and were quickly learning our way around town. Sixteen years later I can't imagine a better place to live.

BOULDER AS A LABORATORY

Boulder is a small city; as of 2012, there are less than 100,000 actual residents with 250,000 people in the extended metro area, which includes the neighboring towns of Superior, Broomfield, Lafayette, Longmont, and Lyons. Boulder is small enough that you can get your mind around the whole place but big enough to be interesting. As a result, I've come to think of Boulder as my laboratory for thinking about startup communities.

Boulder is a smart city. The University of Colorado Boulder is located right in the middle of town, and students, faculty, and staff comprise about 30 percent of the population of Boulder. The presence of several national research labs, including the National Oceanic and Atmospheric Administration (NOAA), the National Center for Atmospheric Research (NCAR), and the National Institute of Standards and Technology (NIST) add nicely to the number of PhDs around. Other alternative education centers, such as Naropa, call Boulder their home.

Although I don't have data to support it, Boulder may have the highest entrepreneurial density in the world. I define entrepreneurial density as follows:

entrepreneurial density = (number of entrepreneurs + number of people working for startups or high growth companies)/adult population.

Boulder's entrepreneurial density, combined with the geographic concentration of entrepreneurial activity around the Boulder downtown core, makes downtown Boulder a hotbed of startup activity.

In 2011, Colorado ranked fourth in the country behind California, Massachusetts, and New York for seed/early-stage dollars invested into startup companies in the state. Although there are not a lot of local venture capital (VC) investors active in Colorado, there are plenty of VCs from around the United States who view companies in Colorado as attractive to invest in, with many of these companies located in Boulder.

Finally, Boulder is an incredibly inclusive community. Although there is some competition between companies, especially over talent, the community is defined by a strong sense of collaboration and philosophy of "giving before you get." If you contribute, you are rewarded, often in unexpected ways. At the same time, especially since it's a small community, it's particularly intolerant of bad actors. If you aren't sincere, constructive, and collaborative, the community behaves accordingly.

Before we dig into the principles of a sustainable startup community, let's spend a little time on the history of Boulder so we can understand how the community evolved.

BEFORE THE INTERNET (1970–1994)

I moved to Boulder in 1995. This, however, was not the beginning of the rise of the startup community in Boulder; the seeds were planted a long time ago and there was a significant amount of entrepreneurial success in and around Boulder between 1970 and 1994. I've asked Kyle Lefkoff, a Boulder resident and venture capitalist since the mid-1970s, to describe what he saw happen during this time frame.

It was not by accident that a university town nestled at the base of the Flatirons would emerge as the densest cluster of technology startups in the world—it was the result of a generation of entrepreneurs drawn to the region first by business necessity, who stayed by choice. Were it not for the foundational success stories in data-storage, pharmaceuticals, and natural-foods brands, Boulder's thriving ecosystem would not exist today. But the success of these anchor tenants presaged the growth and success of today's Boulder startup community.

The data storage landscape was shaped first by IBM's decision to locate its tape-drive division in Boulder in the 1960s, and then, by the success of its first spin off, StorageTek, in 1975. Led by its visionary founders, Jesse Aweida and Juan Rodriguez, StorageTek was Boulder's first big VC-backed high-tech success story, and it spawned a storage and networking industry that grew to dozens of companies by the early 1990s, including billion-dollar success stories such as McData, Exabyte, and Connor Peripherals.

The pharmaceutical industry had its roots in the science laboratories of the University of Colorado's Boulder campus, where a biotech cluster was born from the labs of Marv Caruthers, who founded Amgen and Applied Biosciences, and Larry Gold, who founded Synergen. Together, these successful companies spawned an industry of home-grown biotech companies to compete with Syntex, which based its manufacturing in Boulder, and Ciba-Geigy, which had acquired Geneva Generics, a local generic pill manufacturer. Based on the work of these entrepreneurs, additional pharma successes in this period included Hauser Chemical Research, Somatagen, and Nexstar Pharmaceuticals.

The natural-foods industry began in Boulder with Celestial Seasonings, an herbal tea brand that sprang to national prominence under the leadership of Mo Siegel and Barney Feinblum, who would each go on to play an important role in nearly every other major brand success in the 1980s and early 1990s with Boulder roots, including Alfalfa's, Wild Oats, Whole Foods, Earth's Best Baby Food, Horizon Organic Dairy, and Silk.

A small but devoted group of venture capitalists stood behind these early entrepreneurs and helped put Boulder on the national map of startups. John Hill, a former StorageTek investor, and Carl Carman, a longtime IBM executive, teamed up in the 1980s to form Hill Carman ventures, which backed many of the technology successes in the region. Merc Mercure, the founder of Ball Aerospace, and Bill Coleman, who ran the Syntex facility in Boulder, together formed Colorado Venture Management, the city's first seed fund. Finally, Jim Roser, a renowned East Coast investment banker, moved to Boulder in the 1970s and provided a critical link to capital for a number of local companies. Together, these five individuals pioneered the venture capital industry in Boulder.

Kyle Lefkoff, Boulder Ventures

PRE-INTERNET BUBBLE (1995–2000)

When I first arrived in Boulder, I had no work expectations. At the time I was investing my own money, which I made from the sale of my first company, in startups around the country, and I was spending my time in Boston, New York, San Francisco, and Seattle. Because I was already crisscrossing the country, I figured that having a home base in the middle of the country would make my life easier. Amy and I found Boulder to be beautiful, and, within six months of moving there from Boston, we bought a house just outside of Boulder behind Eldorado Springs State Park, where we still live today.

As I got to know Boulder better, I realized it was perfectly configured for the entrepreneurial revolution that took place around the first wave of the commercial Internet. It was a college town, full of smart, independently minded, and intellectually curious people. As I sat in a bar talking to the one person I knew in town, waiting for Amy to join us for dinner, the guy sitting next to me overheard our conversation and said, "I have a friend who is starting an Internet company. Would you like to meet him?" I did! That person ended up being Andrew Currie, a local entrepreneur who was starting a business with Brian Makare that became Email Publishing, my first Boulder investment. Andrew introduced me to a few of his entrepreneurial friends, and before long I was getting to know the local scene.

I discovered that there was a big divide in Boulder between the entrepreneurs and the investors. Many of the entrepreneurs I met didn't have a lot of respect for the local investors, and as a result, there were a large number of bootstrapped companies. The local investor options for these entrepreneurs were thin as there were only a few small VC firms and these investors tended to be highly selective about who they worked with, often preferring to work with entrepreneurs they'd worked with previously. The newest generation of entrepreneurs who emerged in the mid-1990s had a fierce bias to just do things themselves.

In 1996, I co-founded the Young Entrepreneurs Organization's (YEO) Boulder chapter. I got introductions to a local lawyer, Mike Platt (Cooley), who I still work with today, and a local accountant. I asked each to send out a letter with me to Boulder entrepreneurs they knew to invite them to an inaugural meeting of YEO Boulder. About a dozen people showed up, including Terry Gold (Gold Systems), Paul Berberian (LinkVTC), and Tim Enwall (Solista). Suddenly I was part of a group of a dozen entrepreneurs who were meeting monthly.

In 1997, I co-founded the Colorado Internet Keiretsu. By this point, entrepreneurship around the Internet was growing rapidly, and I was investing aggressively with my new partners at Softbank Technology Ventures in Internet companies across the United States. I put a stake in the ground to organize the Boulder Internet companies and gathered as many founders as I could find at a restaurant in Boulder to discuss building a loose confederation of companies. We repeated this in Denver and then had a large meeting at my house in Eldorado Canyon where everyone discussed a long-term view of putting the region on the map. To this day I'm still working with many of the people who showed up at my house that day.

By 1998 there were several new VC funds in Boulder. Email Publishing was acquired by a public company and became Message Media, which has spawned several other companies over the years. Two of the LinkVTC founders, Paul Berberian and Jim Lejeal, founded Raindance Communications with a third founder, Todd Vernon, each of whom has gone on to start several other companies. Niel Robertson and Rajat Bhargava, both Boston transplants who I had worked with previously at NetGenesis, and Tom Higley, who I had met through his previous company NetDelivery, started Service Metrics, and Exodus acquired it for $280 million 18 months later. Matchlogic, founded by Pete Essler and Ben Addoms and funded by Sequel Ventures, was acquired by Excite. Jared Polis created BlueMountainArts.com, which he sold to Excite for $800 million. Raindance went public. BEA (a large public software company) acquired Avitek, a company started by Tim Miller and Ryan Martens and operated out of the same office as Email Publishing.

Capital was flowing, companies were getting started at a rapid pace, and the energy around startups in Boulder was off the charts. Five years earlier I arrived in Boulder with no expectations about work. Those expectations had changed—I loved Boulder and the entrepreneurial energy. Even though I continued to invest around the country, I increasingly found myself helping build companies close to home.

THE COLLAPSE OF THE INTERNET BUBBLE (2001–2002)

The Internet bubble burst in Boulder, just like it did everywhere else in the world. Suddenly, nothing worked, every company was having layoffs, stock prices of newly public companies were declining precipitously, and capital was nowhere to be found.

Because I invested all around the United States, 2001 was a particularly intense year for me. I was on planes from Monday to Thursday trying to help salvage some of the companies for which I was on the boards. I'd get home Thursday night and spend all day Friday running around Boulder working with my local companies. I'd crash on the weekends and repeat the cycle the following week. At the time, I was on about 25 boards, which, in hindsight, was an insane amount to be trying to handle. I saw Boulder occasionally, and when I did, it was always through the tired eyes of a person simply trying to survive.

Many companies that I was involved in shut their doors in 2001. My failure was a very visible one as layoffs occurred everywhere in my world. I remember working tirelessly to try to help companies get to a sustainable place, but although I was occasionally successful, I failed more often than I succeeded.

Typically, when I have a crappy day, I'll go home, chill out with Amy and my dogs, and resolve to have a better day the next day. By June I realized that every day had been worse than the previous day. So I changed my perspective and decided to simply see what the world had to throw at me. This didn't make things any easier, but my attitude was better, as I continued to grind through the entrepreneurial mess I had made for myself.

I was asleep in the Benjamin Hotel in midtown Manhattan on 9/11/2001 when the first World Trade Center building fell. I had taken a redeye from California the night before, which was pretty typical at that time. I'd get up at 4 A.M. on Monday; take the 6 A.M. flight from Denver to San Francisco to start the week, and then the redeye from San Francisco to New York on Monday or Tuesday night for the rest of the week. I didn't have any meetings until 11 A.M. so I set the clock radio alarm for 9:15 A.M. I woke up to a frantic discussion about a building falling; I thought it was one of the joke NYC drive-time radio stations. As I shook off the cobwebs, I realized it was something serious, turned on the TV, and saw the second tower fall.

My first instinct was to find Amy. She was on her way to the airport in Denver to fly to New York to meet me for a few days, after which we were going to go to Paris for a week of vacation for her birthday. I had turned off my cell phone when I was sleeping so I turned it on and tried to call her but couldn't get through. I dialed directly from the hotel phone and somehow we connected—she was pulled over on the side of the road frantically trying to reach me. Her brain had gone to the horrible thought that I was on one of the planes that had crashed since no one really knew anything yet. After a tearful few minutes, we agreed she should go home and stay put while we sorted out what was going on.

Even though I was 50 blocks away from the World Trade Center, I was terrified. I took a shower and ate some food out of the minibar, but didn't really know what to do. I tried to call Amy again after I got out of the shower, but by now the phones weren't working. I remember looking out the window, on a beautiful Manhattan day, wondering if I should go outside. I decided not to so I fired up my laptop just to see if I could get online. By now the TV was looped on the same information because no one really knew what was happening. Miraculously I got an Internet connection. The West Coast was now awake, so Yahoo! IM and AIM popped up with messages from my partners, entrepreneurs, and friends who knew I was in New York asking if I was okay. My laptop became command central for me for the day since the phones didn't work, marking the first time I can remember the Internet dominating my communication for the day.

At some point, all I wanted to do was get home to Boulder. There were no flights, no cars to rent, and no obvious way to get from New York to Boulder. Eventually I connected with Paul Berberian, the CEO of Raindance, and his CFO, Nick Cuccaro, who also were in New York pitching investors on 9/11. I called my friend Jenny Lawton, who lived in Greenwich, Connecticut, and asked if we could borrow her car. We walked down Park to Grand Central Station, got on an empty train, went to Greenwich, had spaghetti at Jenny's house, and drove the next 28 hours straight until we got home to Boulder.

I then canceled all my travel for the next three months. I marked the fall of 2001 as the end of the Internet bubble for me. I still had a bunch of stuff to clean up, but I made a huge emotional shift at that point and started looking forward instead of looking back. I was happy to be alive and realized that it was unlikely, no matter how messy my world got, that the work I was doing every day would kill me.

This was analogous to the state of the startup community in Boulder post 9/11. Everyone took a giant step back and reevaluated how they were spending their time, what they were spending it on, and why they were spending it that way. Financings came to a halt, along with the creation of new startups. Entrepreneurs and the startup community turned inward and paused.

THE BEGINNING OF THE NEXT WAVE (2003-2011)

By 2003, the seeds of new companies were starting to be planted in Boulder. Experienced entrepreneurs who had made some money pre-Internet bubble weren't done with startups, so many of them started, or started talking about, new businesses. New first-time entrepreneurs started emerging. These entrepreneurs searched out many of the experienced entrepreneurs from the 1990s.

The revolution known as Web 2.0 and the resurgence of the commercial Internet didn't really become visible until 2005, but there were a healthy set of companies being created in Boulder during this time. Although I was still traveling a lot, I'd made a conscious effort to be in Boulder more so I was spending time with Boulder-based companies, such as Rally Software and Return Path. There were plenty of others in which I wasn't invested, like @Last (which was acquired by Google), Tendril, and Webroot that were all growing quickly. The energy in Boulder picked up where it left off, but with a real appreciation for the value of creating substantive companies this time around.

In 2006, David Cohen approached me. He was a successful entrepreneur who had bootstrapped a company called PinPoint Technologies with his partner, David Brown. They sold it to a public company called Zoll Medical. Like many entrepreneurs in Boulder, David had made some money, but he wasn't flashy, was still hungry to do more, and very determined to do it in Boulder. He presented me with an idea he called TechStars that resulted from his frustration as a nascent angel investor. He'd invested in a few companies, written his $25,000 or $50,000 check, and then felt very disconnected from the company he had just invested in. He'd try to help the entrepreneurs, and sometimes he was able to, but often the entrepreneurs didn't want help, didn't know how to ask for help, or were just too busy to focus on engaging David.

This wasn't fulfilling to David, and he assumed there were lots of other angel investors, especially entrepreneurs who had made some money, who also found the "toss some angel money in a company and see what happens" dynamic unsatisfying. So David came up with the idea of helping start a lot more companies by investing a small amount of money in 10 of them at a time, putting them through an intense 90-day program during which they worked closely with mentors and other angel investors to get their businesses to the next stage, at which point they'd be ready to raise a full angel round. This was the core idea at the inception of TechStars.

I immediately loved it. I'd invested much more money in less compelling ideas and figured that the worst case was that we would end up attracting about 30 smart new entrepreneurs to Boulder. In the best case, some new startups would emerge. Either way, we'd have a chance to get a variety of people in the startup community, including experienced entrepreneurs, angels, lawyers, accountants, VCs, and senior members of startup teams, involved in helping these new companies get started.

We ran the first TechStars program in 2007, about the time the Boulder New Tech Meetup got started. Between the two, the summer of 2007 was nonstop software and Internet entrepreneurship in downtown Boulder.

The city was alive with startups, and if there was any question that Boulder had entered a new phase, this confirmed it.

On a national basis, startups around Web 2.0 and social networks began to be visible again. The early success of Facebook, Twitter, LinkedIn, and Zynga generated a renewed interest in web entrepreneurship. Angel investors starting investing their own money into startups, and soon after, VCs started making investments again. Boulder entrepreneurs were the recipients of some of this, and even though there was still a relatively small amount of local VC money in the system, the angels came out in force, especially around TechStars companies. This attracted investors from other parts of the country, which was helped by a steady stream of acquisitions of Boulder-based companies in 2008 and 2009, including SocialThing (by AOL), Filtrbox (by Jive), and RegOnline (by Active).

Today, the Boulder startup scene is one of the best in the United States, certainly for its relatively small size as a city. In addition, Boulder regularly tops many of the best-of lists for a wide variety of topics, including most creative, happiest, healthiest, smartest, and best quality of life (http://start uprev.com/g1). We'll spend a lot of time in this book discussing what drives this, not just in terms of the raw material in the startup community, but the interactions between all the participants, the "give before you get" mentality that leads to strong collaboration, and the broader dynamics at play.

AN OUTSIDER'S VIEW OF BOULDER

Although you've heard my story of how Boulder evolved as a startup community, I thought it would be useful to have an outsider's view of the Boulder startup community. I asked Mark Solon, a general partner at Highway 12 Ventures, a Boise, Idaho–based VC firm to weigh in. Many of Highway 12 Ventures' investments are in Boulder, and Mark has been an active mentor for TechStars since the beginning. Following is his perspective of what's going on in Boulder today.

Since 2000, my partner, Phil Reed, and I have been focused on investing in the most promising startup companies in the Intermountain West. We've invested in terrific companies in Salt Lake City, Tucson, Missoula, Boise, Portland, Seattle, Denver, Albuquerque, Phoenix, and Boise—and spent time in a handful of other cities in the region trying to capitalize on the supply-demand imbalance of good ideas versus capital in all of these terrific startup towns that get largely overlooked by the vast majority of venture capitalists.

All of these communities have both advantages and disadvantages for startups to thrive—and each have fostered important and lasting companies that grew from their respective startup ecosystems. None, however, has come close to producing anywhere near the volume of successful startups, especially on a per-capita basis, as Boulder. For the last decade, Boulder has produced successful startups at an astonishing rate. Why is that?

Many will point to TechStars as the primary reason, but that's the easy answer. TechStars has indeed become a global phenomenon, and the impact on Boulder has been significant. However, we started investing in Boulder companies before anyone had ever heard of David Cohen or TechStars.

It's my belief that Boulder is unique because the entrepreneurs and other participants in Boulder's startup ecosystem have a greater sense of community than anywhere else in the country. The ethos of mentorship and support by the people who comprise Boulder's startup community were firmly in place when TechStars arrived in 2007. David Cohen's brilliant idea was merely the lightning rod that sparked one of the greatest job-creation engines our country has ever seen.

In Boulder, people are willing to work harder and devote a greater amount of time to help startups succeed with no expectations for reward. Notice that I didn't say they care more than elsewhere, since most cities take pride and care about the success of their startups. However, I've never seen another community reach out and devote as much time, passion, and hard work at helping startups as in Boulder.

I'll never forget one of my early visits to Boulder. After a full day of meeting with startups, I was asked by the entrepreneurs I was with if I'd like to join them and some peers for a "special dinner." "Sure," I replied. "What's special about it?" "It's a wake," they deadpanned. That dinner showed me that the fabric of this small mountain town was different than anywhere else I'd been. Turns out that, earlier that week, a local startup had decided to shut down and the "wake" was the startup community's way of showing these young, fragile entrepreneurs that it was okay to fail—that the honor was in trying. They made those founders feel good about themselves in a moment that was critical in their development as entrepreneurs. As an aside, in this case the founders didn't run out of money. After giving it their best effort, they realized their business wasn't going to be the great success they had envisioned, and they decided to return their remaining cash to their investors. The epilogue of that dinner is that the founders had roles at other local startups within a few weeks.

The biggest observation I can offer from having a front row seat to seeing Boulder becoming one of the hottest startup markets in the United States over the last decade is that there was no strategic plan. Government had little to do with it and there weren't committees wading in bureaucratic quicksand wasting hundreds of hours of people's time strategizing about how to create more startups. Boulder caught fire because a few dozen entrepreneurs believed in their hearts that a rising tide lifts all boats and they derived great pleasure from helping make that happen.

This can happen in any community in the country. All it takes is a small group of credible people to lead by example. People like Paul Berberian, Todd Vernon, Jim Franklin, Ari Newman, Tim Enwall, and Howard Diamond. These folks, despite having full-time jobs as founders of growing companies, regularly devote large chunks of their time to assist the next wave of startups, which help make Boulder the very special place it is.

Mark Solon, Highway 12 Ventures, @mark_solon

As you can see, the Boulder startup community has evolved over a long period of time, with the seeds being planted in the 1970s. Numerous entrepreneurs have been involved in its creation, growth, and ongoing development. By 2012, many of the entrepreneurs who are active as leaders today were involved in various phases of the Boulder startup community dating back 20 years. These entrepreneurs are still involved, and you can expect them to continue to lead for the foreseeable future. As Mark Solon asserts, the magic comes from a few dozen entrepreneurs deciding that the success of the greater startup community is worth their investment of time and energy.

CHAPTER THREE

PRINCIPLES OF A VIBRANT STARTUP COMMUNITY

Now that you've had an introduction to Boulder and its history from my point of view, I'd like to describe the principles that drive the Boulder startup community, which I'll call the Boulder Thesis. First, however, I'll discuss the three historical frameworks that have been used to describe why some cities become vibrant startup communities.

HISTORICAL FRAMEWORKS

The investigation into startup communities is among the most important inquiries of our time. Why do some places flourish with innovation while others wither? What are the determinants that help a startup community achieve critical startup mass? Once under way, how does a startup community sustain and expand entrepreneurship? Why do startup communities persist, despite often having higher real estate costs and wages than other areas? At stake is nothing less than the continued economic vitality, and even the very existence of towns, cities, and regions.

Studies show that the geography of innovation is neither democratic nor flat. This may be surprising since you might think that location should matter less than ever in today's society. Information can be quickly sent and received by anyone from almost anywhere. In theory, expanding access to resources and information from anywhere might decouple the relationship between place and innovation.

Economic geographers, however, observe the opposite effect. Evidence suggests that location, rather than being irrelevant, is more important than ever. Innovation tilts heavily toward certain locations and, as scholar Richard Florida (professor at Rotman School of Management, at the University of Toronto and author of *The Rise of the Creative Class* (2002)) says, is "spiky" with great concentration of creative, innovative people in tightly clustered geographies. Location clearly matters.

Three prominent frameworks explain why some locales are hotbeds of entrepreneurship whereas others are the innovation equivalent of a twenty-first century economic mirage. Each explanation of regional entrepreneurial advantage comes from a different discipline—one from economics, another from sociology, and a third from geography. These explanations are, for the most part, nonexclusive and complementary.

The first explanation, *external or agglomeration economies*, comes from economics. This line of analysis reaches back to the research of economist Alfred Marshall, and, in recent decades, Michael Porter, Paul Krugman, and Paul Romer have deepened this account. External economies focus on the benefits of startup concentration in an area. This explanation focuses on economic concepts as they apply to location. One is that companies co-located in an area benefit from "external economies of scale." Emerging companies need certain common inputs—for example, infrastructure, specialized legal and accounting services, suppliers, labor pools with a specialized knowledge base—that reside outside the company. Companies in a common geographic area share the fixed costs of these resources external to the company. As more and more startups in an area can share the costs of specialized inputs, the average cost per startup drops for the specialized inputs. This provides direct economic benefit to companies located within a startup community.

Another economic concept, *network effects*, explains why geographic concentration yields further advantage. Network effects operate in systems where the addition of a member to a network enhances value for existing users. The Internet, Facebook, and Twitter are examples in which network effects operate powerfully. These services may have some value to you if there are just 100 other users. However, these networks are immensely more useful if there are 100 million other users that you can connect with. Startup communities similarly feature strong network effects. For example, an area with 10 great programmers provides a valuable pool of labor talent for a startup. However, an additional 1,000 amazing programmers in the same area is vastly more valuable to startups, especially if programmers share best practices with other programmers, inspire one another, or start new companies. External economies of scale lower certain costs; meanwhile, network effects make co-location more valuable.

The second explanation of startup communities, *horizontal networks*, comes from sociology. In her PhD work at MIT, AnnaLee Saxenian (currently Dean of the UC Berkeley School of Information) noticed that external economies do not fully explain the development and adaptation of startup communities. In particular, in her seminal book *Regional Advantage: Culture and Competition in Silicon Valley and Route 128* (1994) Saxenian noted that two hotbeds for high-tech activity—Silicon Valley and Boston's Route 128—looked very similar in the mid-1980s. Each area enjoyed agglomeration economies associated with the nation's two high-tech regions. Yet just a decade later, Silicon Valley gained a dominant advantage over Route 128. External economies alone did not provide an answer. Saxenian set out to resolve the puzzle of why Silicon Valley far outpaced Route 128 from the mid-1980s to mid-1990s.

Saxenian persuasively argues that a culture of openness and information exchange fueled Silicon Valley's ascent over Route 128. This argument is tied to network effects, which are better leveraged by a community with a culture of information sharing across companies and industries. Saxenian observed that the porous boundaries between Silicon Valley companies, such as Sun Microsystems and HP, stood in stark contrast to the closed-loop and autarkic companies of Route 128, such as DEC and Apollo. More broadly, Silicon Valley culture embraced a horizontal exchange of information across and between companies. Rapid technological disruption played perfectly to Silicon Valley's culture of open information exchange and labor mobility. As technology quickly changed, the Silicon Valley companies were better positioned to share information, adopt new trends, leverage innovation, and nimbly respond to new conditions. Meanwhile, vertical integration and closed systems disadvantaged many Route 128 companies during periods of technological upheaval. Saxenian highlights the role of a densely networked culture in explaining Silicon Valley's successful industrial adaptation as compared to Route 128.

Finally, the third explanation of startup communities, the notion of the *creative class*, comes from geography. Richard Florida describes the tie between innovation and creative-class individuals. The creative class is composed of individuals such as entrepreneurs, engineers, professors, and artists who create "meaningful new forms." Creative-class individuals, Florida argues, want to live in nice places, enjoy a culture with a tolerance for new ideas and weirdness, and—most of all—want to be around other creative-class individuals. This is another example of network effects, because a virtuous cycle exists where the existence of a creative class in an area attracts more creative-class individuals to the area, which in turn makes the area even more valuable and attractive. A location that hits critical mass enjoys a competitive geographic advantage over places that have yet to attract a significant number of creative-class individuals.

Each of the three explanations just outlined provides a useful lens to understand why the entrepreneurial world has concentrations of startup communities in specific geographies. They are incomplete, how-ever, concerning how to put a startup community into motion. There is a serious chicken and egg problem; although it is not difficult to see why inno-vation havens have an advantage, it is more challenging to explain how to get a startup community up and running.

THE BOULDER THESIS

I suggest a fourth framework based on our experience in Boulder. Let's call it the Boulder Thesis. This framework has four key components:

1. Entrepreneurs must lead the startup community.
2. The leaders must have a long-term commitment.
3. The startup community must be inclusive of anyone who wants to participate in it.
4. The startup community must have continual activities that engage the entire entrepreneurial stack.

LED BY ENTREPRENEURS

The most critical principle of a startup community is that entrepreneurs must lead it. Lots of different people are involved in the startup community and many nonentrepreneurs play key roles. Unless the entrepreneurs lead, the startup community will not be sustainable over time.

In virtually every major city, there are long lists of different types of people and organizations who are involved in the startup community includ-ing government, universities, investors, mentors, and service providers. Historically, many of these organizations try to play a leadership role in the development of their local startup community. Although their involvement is important, they can't be the leaders. The entrepreneurs have to be leaders.

I define an entrepreneur as someone who has co-founded a company. I differentiate between "high-growth entrepreneurial companies" and "small businesses." Both are important, but they are different things. Entrepreneurial companies have the potential to be or are high-growth businesses whereas small businesses tend to be local, profitable, but slow-growth organizations. Small-business people are often "pillars of their community" as their businesses have a tight co-dependency with their community. By contrast, founders of high-growth entrepreneurial companies generally are involved in the local community as employers and indirect contributors to small businesses and the local economy, but they rarely are involved in the broad business community because they are extraordinarily focused on their companies.

Because of this intense focus, it's unrealistic to think that all entrepreneurs in a community will be leaders. All that is needed is a critical mass of entrepreneurs, often less than a dozen, who will provide leadership.

LONG-TERM COMMITMENT

These leaders have to make a long-term commitment to their startup community. I like to say this has to be at least 20 years from today to reinforce the sense that this has to be meaningful in length. Optimally, the commitment resets daily; it should be a forward-looking 20-year commitment.

It's well understood that economies run in cycles. Economies grow, peak, decline, bottom out, grow again, peak again, decline again, and bottom out again. Some of these cycles are modest. Some are severe. The lengths vary dramatically.

Startup communities have to take a very long-term view. A great startup community such as Silicon Valley (1950–today) has a long trajectory. Although they have their booms and busts, they continued to grow, develop, and expand throughout this period of time.

Most cities and their leaders get excited about entrepreneurship after a major economic decline. They focus on it for a few years through a peak.

When the subsequent decline ultimately happens, they focus on other things during the downturn. When things bottom out, most of the progress gained during the upswing was lost. I've seen this several times—first in the early 1990s and again around the Internet bubble. All you have to do is think back to the nickname of your city during the Internet bubble (Silicon Alley, Silicon Swamp, Silicon Slopes, Silicon Prairie, Silicon Gulch, and Silicon Mountain) to remember what it was like before and after the peak.

This is why the leaders have to first be entrepreneurs and then have a long-term view. These leaders must be committed to the continuous development of their startup community, regardless of the economic cycle their city, state, or country is in. Great entrepreneurial companies, such as Apple, Genentech, Microsoft, and Intel, were started during down economic cycles. It takes such a long time to create something powerful that, almost by definition, you'll go through several economic cycles on the path to glory.

If you aspire to be a leader of your startup community, but you aren't willing to live where you are for the next 20 years and work hard at leading the startup community for that period of time, ask yourself what your real motivation for being a leader is. Although you can have impact for a shorter period of time, it'll take at least this level of commitment from some leaders to sustain a vibrant startup community.

FOSTER A PHILOSOPHY OF INCLUSIVENESS

A startup community must be extremely inclusive. Anyone who wants to engage should be able to, whether they are changing careers, moving to your city, graduating from college, or just want to do something different. This applies to entrepreneurs, people who want to work for startups, people who want to work with startups, or people who are simply intellectually interested in startups.

This philosophy of inclusiveness applies at all levels of the startup community. The leaders have to be open to having more leaders involved, recognizing that leaders need to be entrepreneurs who have a long-term view of building their startup community. Entrepreneurs in the community need to welcome other entrepreneurs, viewing the growth of the startup community as a positive force for all, rather than a zero-sum game in which new entrepreneurs compete locally for resources and status. Employees of startups need to recruit their friends and open their homes and city to other people who have moved into the community.

Everyone in the startup community should have a perspective that having more people engaged in the startup community is good for the startup community. Building a startup community is not a zero-sum game in which there are winners and losers; if everyone engages, they and the entire community can all be winners.

ENGAGE THE ENTIRE ENTREPRENEURIAL STACK

Startup communities must have regular activities that engage the entire entrepreneurial stack. This includes first-time entrepreneurs, experienced entrepreneurs, aspiring entrepreneurs, investors, mentors, employees of startups, service providers to startups, and anyone else who wants to be involved.

Over the years, I've been to many entrepreneurial award events, periodic cocktail parties, monthly networking events, panel discussions, and open houses. Although these types of activities have a role, typically in shining a bright light on the people doing good things within the startup community, they don't really engage anyone in any real entrepreneurial activity.

The emergence of hackathons, new tech meetups, open coffee clubs, startup weekends, and accelerators like TechStars stand out in stark contrast. These are activities and events, which I will cover in depth later in this book, that last from a few hours to three months and provide a tangible, focused, set of activities for the members of the startup community to engage in. By being inclusive of the startup community, these activities consistently engage the entire entrepreneurial stack.

Some of these activities will last for decades; others will go strong for a few years and then fade away; others will fail to thrive and die quickly. This dynamic is analogous to startups—it's okay to try things that fail, and the startup community must recognize when something isn't working and move on. The leaders of the failed activity should try again to create things that engage the entire entrepreneurial stack, and participants in failed activities should keep on engaging in stuff, recognizing that they are playing a long-term game.

CHAPTER FOUR

PARTICIPANTS IN A STARTUP COMMUNITY

eaders of startup communities have to be entrepreneurs. Everyone else is a feeder into the startup community. Both leaders and feeders are important, but their roles are different.

Leaders of a startup community must have a long-term commitment, welcome everyone to the startup community, and help create things that engage the entire entrepreneurial stack. Over 20 years, it's likely that each entrepreneur will go through different phases in his company, have success and failure, start new companies, and work with many different people. Although many things in the entrepreneurs' lives will change, they have to stay focused on providing leadership to their startup community or else they shouldn't commit to this leadership role in the first place.

There are many different leadership roles within the startup community. Some leaders take on a specific role, like Tim Enwall, the founder of Tendril, as one of the leaders of Colorado Startup Summer. Others have broad influence through their actual business, as David Cohen does as CEO of TechStars. And others, like Robert Reich, the co-founder of OpenSpace, engage a broad cross-section by creating and hosting the Boulder Denver New Tech Meetup.

Leaders set an example. They are tireless in their evangelism for their startup community, put their community and geography ahead of their self-interest, and just do stuff. By taking action, they provide authority for others to become leaders.

There is no "leader of the leaders." The best startup communities are loosely organized and consist of broad, evolving networks of people. By having inclusive philosophies, it's very easy for new leaders to emerge organically. Furthermore, there are no votes, no hierarchy, no titles, and no specific roles. Since the leaders are entrepreneurs, they are used to ambiguity as well as a rapid and continuous evolution of the community.

I like to think of a startup community as an evolving organism, rather than a well-defined structure. Once the organism starts evolving, as long as it retains its inclusive gene, it will continue to evolve as new leaders get into the mix.

Feeders are everyone else in the startup community. This includes government, universities, investors, mentors, service providers, and large companies. I'll describe each of these, and their corresponding roles, in more detail shortly.

Historically, many of the feeders thought of themselves as leaders. This has been one of the primary inhibitors of the long-term growth and evolution of many startup communities. These feeders run on different time cycles (e.g., the two- or four-year cycle of government) or have different motivations (i.e., service providers grow by generating increasing revenue from clients) than the entrepreneurs in the startup community. Although this misalignment may seem minor, it has a huge negative impact on the evolution of the startup community when in a leadership role.

It's important to realize that being a feeder is not a bad thing. Rather, it's a clear description of the specific role. The startup community wouldn't be successful over the long term without both leaders and feeders. However, the absence of entrepreneurs as leaders, or the overwhelming leadership by feeders, will doom a startup community.

ENTREPRENEURS

The leaders of a startup community must be the entrepreneurs. These entrepreneurs must have a long-term commitment to their startup community. They must be inclusive of anyone who wants to engage with the startup community. They must be actively involved—they have to show up, do, and lead by example. Finally, they have to put the long-term health of the startup community ahead of their self-interests.

At the beginning of its arc, a startup community needs only a few leaders. In Boulder, I can point to half a dozen people that ignited the entrepreneurial revolution the city has been enjoying. Over time, the number of leaders grows, roles change, and some leaders take a backseat to other leaders. This is critical; without evolution, the startup community will stagnate.

Entrepreneurs are extremely busy running their companies. Many entrepreneurs have families and struggle mightily with balancing their work and the rest of their life. "Leading their startup community" can sound like one more burden on top of an already overwhelming set of responsibilities. However, some entrepreneurs figure out how to do it. How?

Any entrepreneur who has been a leader of a startup community knows the incredible amount of energy to be gained from other entrepreneurs. These entrepreneurial leaders follow a "give before you get" philosophy: They have no idea what they are going to get out of providing this leadership, but they expect it will be more than they invest. In some cases, the results are tangible and immediate; in other cases the results are vague and take a long time to materialize. Regardless, the short-term emotional satisfaction of helping to mobilize, grow, and evolve a startup community is substantial.

Entrepreneurial leaders are charismatic. People want to be around them and are inspired by them. I don't believe that people motivate other people; rather they create a context in which others are motivated. Some entrepreneurs are spectacular at creating this context, and when they lead by example, many other entrepreneurs rise to the occasion. This phenomenon is self-reinforcing; I've seen it happen in Boulder and it is incredibly powerful once it reaches critical mass.

The startup community is always evolving. If the entrepreneurial leaders try to control this evolution, they will fail and undermine their previous efforts. Instead, entrepreneurial leaders should embrace this evolution, encourage and support new things, people, and ideas, and recognize that other entrepreneurs' leadership is additive to the system. Rather than view it as a zero-sum game, in which there's a leader on top, they view it as a game with increasing returns, in which the larger the number of entrepreneurs involved, the more great things happen.

GOVERNMENT

When I'm talking to groups about startup communities, one of the questions I ask is, "How many of you are entrepreneurs?" If less than half the audience consists of entrepreneurs, there is a fundamental problem. I've been in situations in which, after I've asked, "How many of you are entrepreneurs or investors—angel or VC?" still less than half of the hands went up. In one case, this was less than a quarter of the hands. When I started going around the room and asking the rest of the people for titles, they were things like city economic development director, state office of economic development, northwest state regional development director, and mayor's office of business development. Twenty-five people later, I asked each of them to stop and then turned to the entrepreneurs and said, "Please give me specific examples of how these people have helped you with your business." None were forthcoming.

In general, state and local governments, at least in the United States, are well intentioned. So, when you think of government as a feeder into your startup community, take an optimistic and constructive view. Recognize that there are a number of barriers that people in government have to overcome to be effective in a startup community.

For starters, the cadence of government is out of sync with a long-term view. Government runs in short time cycles, usually less than four years. It often feels like we are in an endless campaign cycle and, in some cases, at least half of the activity of government leaders feels like it is around the process of getting reelected. After an election, there is often a three-month lame-duck period where nothing happens, followed by a six-month period as the new administration gears up, puts new leaders in place, makes its plans, does its studies, writes its reports, and then launches its new initiatives. That's nine months of a four-year cycle wasted. Startup communities can't wait—they are growing and changing every day.

It is well known that government can inhibit business activity. The easy things to pin on government are overwhelming regulatory activity, misguided tax policy that stalls investment in entrepreneurial companies, shortsighted tax policy that drives entrepreneurial companies to neighboring cities or states, and constrictive zoning rules, especially in downtown cores, that drive rents up and lower inventory of office and living space. At the minimum, these types of behavior make state and local government look stupid to entrepreneurs and directly contradict the entrepreneurs-are-important message that government often is trying to get out there.

Other state laws, like those around noncompete agreements, stifle entrepreneurial activity. Historically, noncompete agreements were viewed as necessary to protect employers and companies. However, noncompete agreements have long been unenforceable in California and are often cited as one of the drivers of the health of the Silicon Valley entrepreneurial ecosystem.

Many government employees don't understand entrepreneurship. When I first started trying to understand government's role in entrepreneurship, I agreed to co-chair the Colorado Governor's Innovation Council under then-Governor Bill Ritter. The first thing I realized is that few people I encountered in local or state government understood the difference between small businesses and high-growth entrepreneurial businesses. When I explored this at a federal level, it was just as bad; the Small Business Administration is responsible for both, and it's telling that its name is the Small Business Administration rather than the High-Growth Business Administration.

Government exists to support, yet many local and state governments believe they can create. This is true in good economic times when government is investing in growth and in bad economic times when government is cutting back, yet investing in recovery. Government is great at shining a bright light on things and using its bully pulpit to stimulate agendas, but it is terrible at investing in and creating new entrepreneurial activity. This is true at both the state level and the local level. However, if you work for city government or for the mayor's office, and your title is Economic Development Liaison or Small Business Development Director, by definition you believe your job is to help companies grow.

Of course, there are things government can do to help the startup community grow, but from a support role rather than a leadership role. I've found these to vary dramatically by startup community. As a result, I always encourage government people to ask the entrepreneurs what they need. Once you've asked, you have a choice. You can say, "We aren't able to do that" or "excellent idea—we are going to go do that now." The worst thing you can do is to be in the middle with entrepreneurs.

Finally, if you work for the government and are excited about entrepreneurship, don't be afraid to engage deeply as a participant in the startup community. This will be after hours and on weekends, just like everyone else. But you'll be welcomed. And who knows, you might decide to be an entrepreneur.

UNIVERSITIES

There is a strong conventional belief that for a startup community to be successful, it has to be located close to a major university. The two regularly cited examples of this are MIT's proximity to Cambridge/Boston/Route 128 and Stanford's proximity to Silicon Valley. Although a university presence is valuable to a startup community, I reject the premise that the startup community is dependent on the university. It's from this perspective that I categorize universities as feeders to the startup community.

Universities have five resources relevant to entrepreneurship: students, professors, research labs, entrepreneurship programs, and technology transfer offices. The first two resources, which are people, are much more important than the last three, which are institutions. The idea that people are always more important than institutions is fundamental to creating a healthy startup community.

Students are by far the most important contribution of a university to a startup community. Every year, a new crop of eager freshmen arrive on campus. Some of these freshmen are destined to become entrepreneurs; others will work for startups. Regardless of what they end up doing, they all bring new ideas and fresh perspectives to the community. Additionally, each year brings new graduate students to the community. These graduate students are almost always a net positive contribution to the intellectual capacity of the community. Some will engage in entrepreneurship, either through starting companies around the work they are doing or joining startups that are interesting to them. In each case, new blood in the system is powerful.

Professors come next in importance. In universities that have a culture of entrepreneurship, many professors themselves are entrepreneurs. In some situations this entrepreneurial activity is around their own research; in others they are simply captivated by ideas from their students and join in on the entrepreneurial journey as co-founders, advisors, and mentors. Sometimes the fundamental innovation comes from professors, but often the professors merely create a context for an independent thinker to come up with something new and amazing.

Research labs are also a part of this. A university like MIT is specifically oriented around departments (e.g., Course 6–Computer Science and Electrical Engineering) and labs (e.g., Computer Science and Artificial Intelligence Laboratory [CSAIL] and the Media Lab). Professors from multiple departments participate in the labs—some spend more time teaching; others spend more time on research—but the intersection of the academic programs with the research labs creates a powerful petri dish for entrepreneurial activities.

Many universities have entrepreneurship programs. These programs are often located in the business school, which is exactly the wrong place for them. This dynamic emerged from the notion that you could teach entrepreneurship, an idea that is heavily debated both inside and outside academia. Having a formal entrepreneurship program is powerful, especially in the context of linking the university to the startup community, but for the program to be effective it should be juxtaposed with the students and professors creating new innovations. In most cases, this innovation is outside the business school—in engineering, computer science, life science departments, and the labs. By putting the entrepreneurship center in the business school, a university creates a dynamic by which the business people wait for the innovators to come to them, while the innovators are heads down in their labs, in front of their computers and with their colleagues, hard at work at all hours of the day and night. To change this, I encourage the business school students interested in entrepreneurship to go out across the campus and find the inventors, rather than wait for the inventors to come to them. Forward-looking universities realize this and put the entrepreneurship center on the other side of campus from the business school.

The Bayh-Dole Act of 1980 sparked the creation of the technology transfer office at universities, and fulfilled the vision of Vannevar Bush dating back to 1945. Today, technology transfer offices (TTOs) are ubiquitous at virtually all universities that have any kind of research activities. In many cases, TTOs are helpful in the process of licensing university research to new startups. However, in many situations they are toxic because of absurd licensing terms; excessive requests for equity or royalties; difficult licensing and contracting practices; and overreaching, restrictive IP protection that inhibits innovation. In some cases, the TTO is tightly integrated into the fabric of the university; in others it is a separate organization with a clear mission to generate as much revenue as possible through the capture and licensing of IP. I encourage all universities to look west toward the leadership of Stanford as an example, and the corresponding impact on the Silicon Valley startup community.

I'm often asked how universities can better engage with the startup community. As a feeder, the university can be a great convener of entrepreneurial activities. Universities have great spaces to work, large conference and auditorium facilities, and lots of students and faculty interested in entrepreneurship. We've seen this play out brilliantly in Boulder through the leadership of CU Law and the Silicon Flatirons program. Although the law school is an unlikely place to envision the core entrepreneurial activity in the university, several of the leaders at CU Law, including the now Dean Phil Weiser and Brad Bernthal, have taken it upon themselves to provide leadership across the university. CU Law and Silicon Flatirons host a steady stream of entrepreneurial activities and groups, including the Boulder Denver New Tech Meetup, regular national conferences on entrepreneurship, and the entrepreneurial law clinic, which provides free legal support from law school students to the Boulder-based startup companies. In addition, the CU New Venture Challenge, a cross-campus new business competition, started at CU Law and results in a focal point for cross-campus entrepreneurial activity. There are many things CU Boulder could do better around entrepreneurship, but the role of CU as a convener for entrepreneurial activity is demonstrated extremely well by the role of CU Law and Silicon Flatirons.

Finally, the culture of the university plays a critically important role in how it engages with the startup community. Again, MIT and Stanford are excellent examples of this. As you walk down the halls, you see professors who are founders of multibillion-dollar companies, in some cases multiple times. They work out of modest offices like everyone else, engage deeply with students, and are incredibly passionate about the work they do academically and entrepreneurially. Their institutions respect and support these outside activities, and they provide strong entrepreneurial role models for their peers and students. Finally, some of the wealth created often cycles back to the university, either through licensing via the TTO, or more notably, through major gifts these professors and their co-founders give back to the university after their companies succeed.

Remember, universities are a source of fresh blood, new thinking, and additional potential leaders to your startup community. If you look at the startup communities around MIT and Stanford, you see an ever-evolving cast of entrepreneurs who came from these schools providing intellectual, emotional, and functional leadership for the startup community over a long period of time. Embrace and include the university, but don't rely on it to lead.

INVESTORS

Although investors are a key part of a startup community, they are often inappropriately blamed for the failure of a startup community to thrive, or excessively praised for a startup community's success. The phrase "there is not enough capital here for startups" is heard all over the world, and it is as much of a cliché as "money will go to where the good deals are." At the early stage, raising money is hard, figuring out which deals are good is hard, and everything else associated with getting a company up and running is hard, so what's the big deal? Rather than struggle with this, investors should recognize that they are feeders into the startup community, play a long-term game, and work hard to help support the development of their startup communities.

One of the classic problems is that some investors view themselves as gatekeepers to a startup community. This is especially true at the early stages where investors, especially local VC firms, position themselves as the first source of smart capital. When I moved to Boulder in the mid-1990s, I often heard from other local VCs things like "we invest in the best local deals and then import out-of-state investors for the next rounds." Although true in some cases, the dependency is an unhealthy one, especially when there are very few local VCs or the investors they import from out of state end up with crummy financial results over time.

Investor arrogance is tightly coupled to this. Many investors forget that the entrepreneurs are doing all the really hard work. Whenever investors start talking about "my entrepreneurs" or "my companies," you know you have a problem. In the context of the long-term development of a startup community, this investor arrogance can be destructive if it polarizes an already fragile relationship between the entrepreneur and investor.

When I refer to investors, I'm lumping angels and VCs together in the same category. In some cases, their roles overlap, but there can be fundamental differences in how they operate. For example, VCs are in business to invest money in equity and generate economic returns for themselves and their investors. That's it. Although angels have the same goal, their individual motivations, especially on a deal-by-deal basis, may be more nuanced. Furthermore, VCs are not all the same; there are many different behavioral archetypes. These differences are important in the context of the health of a startup community. Goal alignment over the long term is important, and it is yet another reason why investors fall into the category of feeders because these goals are driven by the entrepreneurs and supported by the investors.

There are exceptions. When you look around different startup communities, you see VCs playing an effective leadership role. In New York, Fred Wilson at Union Square Ventures immediately comes to mind. In Los Angeles, it is Mark Suster at GRP. However, the examples are few and far between. Fundamentally, a VC can't declare him- or herself a leader of a startup community; he or she must earn this over a long period of time through deep commitment, effort, and involvement in the startup community.

MENTORS

Mentors are experienced entrepreneurs or investors who actively contribute time, energy, and wisdom to startups and can be a key part of a startup community.

Often the terms *advisor* and *mentor* are conflated. An advisor has an economic relationship with the company he is advising. In contrast, a mentor doesn't. The mentor is helping startups without a clear set of outcome goals or economic rewards. I refer to this as a "give before you get" approach. Mentors are counting on their contribution of good karma coming back around at some point, in some way, without a predefined expectation.

For a mentor to be successful, there are a number of things to consider. At TechStars, we've created a mentor manifesto, which follows and explains many of the key behaviors of a mentor (http://startuprev.com/g2).

- Be Socratic.
- Expect nothing in return (you'll be delighted with what you do get back).
- Be authentic/practice what you preach.
- Be direct. Tell the truth, however hard.
- Listen, too.
- The best mentor relationships eventually become two-way relationships.
- Be responsive.
- Adopt at least one company every single year. Experience counts.

- Clearly separate opinion from fact.
- Hold information in confidence.
- Clearly commit to mentor or do not. Either is fine.
- Know what you don't know. Say, "I don't know" when you don't know. "I don't know" is preferable to bravado.
- Guide, don't control. Teams must make their own decisions. Guide but never tell them what to do. Understand that it's their company, not yours.
- Accept and communicate with other mentors that get involved.
- Be optimistic.
- Provide specific actionable advice; don't be vague.
- Be challenging/robust but never destructive.
- Have empathy. Remember that startups are hard.

The most powerful mentor/mentee relationships are those in which the mentor and the mentee ultimately become peers. In many situations, the mentor often learns more from the mentee. At some moment in time, they become mentors to each other.

SERVICE PROVIDERS

Every startup community has service providers. These are the lawyers, accountants, recruiters, marketing consultants, and contract CFOs who help startups in many different ways. Some of these service providers are significant companies; others are individual consultants.

The best service providers invest their time and energy for no charge in early-stage companies. As these companies develop, the service providers are rewarded with long-term business relationships with fast-growing companies. In some cases, smart service providers will invest in early rounds, and occasionally the returns from these equity investments can dwarf the fees paid to the firm over time.

In addition to focusing energy on the startups, great service providers can help with the growth of the startup community. Many of the more established firms have marketing budgets that can underwrite entrepreneurship events or they have physical infrastructure, such as a large office, which can be used to host startup events. Some partners at law or accounting firms love working with startups at the very early stages and often have broad networks that can be brought to the table. In all cases, if the service provider is taking a long-term view and looking past the next monthly fee, it can have a very positive impact on the development of the community.

Some service providers and consultants are in it just for the money. These firms don't understand the "give before you get" philosophy and tend not to be helpful. In some cases they negatively impact the startup community and over time are alienated by the startup community. If they are individual consultants, they often disappear from the scene and take a job somewhere. If they are firms, they'll often continue to have business in the community, but rarely do they become the go-to firm for startups.

LARGE COMPANIES

Large companies can play an important role in any startup community. However, there is often much confusion, from both entrepreneurs and the employees of the large companies, about what an effective set of activities is.

The two most powerful things large companies can do for the startup community are (1) provide a convening space and resources for local startups, and (2) create programs to encourage startups to build companies that enhance the large company's ecosystem.

In Boulder, Google does an awesome job of providing its space for startups. It has a fun office in an old Circuit City building and has created an event space that comfortably holds 250 people. This space is free to any local gathering of entrepreneurs as long as they arrange it in advance with the folks at Google. It's a generous offer, and it allows Boulder Google employees to easily engage with startup activity in Boulder that they are interested in, while creating goodwill for Google within the Boulder startup community.

On an international basis, Microsoft has created a program called Bizspark, which began five years ago by providing free Microsoft software to startups. It has expanded greatly since then, now including an accelerator program (run by TechStars), international publicity for "Bizspark startups," free hosting infrastructure via Azure, and deep access to key Microsoft product groups for startups that are building technologies that enhance the Microsoft ecosystem.

Many large companies are standoffish to the startup community. They worry that if they engage, the startups they interact with will recruit their employees. Although this can happen, having the opportunity to interact with startups enhances the quality of the employee's job. This often increases job satisfaction and long-term employee retention.

THE IMPORTANCE OF BOTH LEADERS AND FEEDERS

Startup communities need both leaders and feeders. The problem comes when the feeders try to lead or when there is an absence of leaders.

If the startup community has a culture of inclusiveness, it will constantly have entrepreneurs step up into leadership positions. The existing leaders need to be welcoming of these new leaders or else the startup community will have the "patriarch problem," which I'll describe later. The entrepreneurial leaders also need to be inclusive of any feeders who want to participate.

It's hard to separate interest from action. Because building a startup community is a long-term commitment, leaders can easily engage new leaders and feeders by giving them assignments. These assignments can be simple at first, but by giving people tangible things to do, you quickly separate people who are willing to engage from those who merely are looking to network or simply get something from the startup community. Always remember the mindset of "give before you get," and challenge anyone who wants to engage in the startup community to demonstrate this with their actions.

Finally, every startup community needs cheerleaders. These cheerleaders are both the leaders and the feeders, because everyone in the community should be proud of what they are doing and shout it from the rooftops. This cheerleading can be via a community web site, such as what exists in Washington, DC (http://startuprev.com/b0), Chicago (http://startuprev.com/j0), and nationally (http://startuprev.com/n0), or it can be the regular, steady blogging, writing, and talking that we have in Boulder by the individual leaders and feeders. Regardless, be proud of what you are doing in your community, and make noise about it to the world.

CHAPTER FIVE

ATTRIBUTES OF LEADERSHIP IN A STARTUP COMMUNITY

There are four key attributes to leadership in a startup community. The leaders must be inclusive. They must realize they are not playing a zero-sum game. They need to be mentorship driven and recognize the continual power of a mentor-mentee relationship. Finally, they must embrace porous boundaries. I'll explore these in more detail in this chapter.

BE INCLUSIVE

For the leaders of a startup community to be effective, they need to be inclusive. Anyone, regardless of experience, background, education, ethnicity, or perspective should be welcomed into the startup community if they want to engage with it.

Leaders have a special role in this process. People who want to get involved in a startup community approach them first. These people might be moving from another city, working for a large company, graduating from college, or simply be interested in getting more involved in what's going on in the startup community. The leaders are the gatekeepers and should make sure the gates are always open.

When someone new shows up at the gates of a startup community, the leaders should do a few things. First, they should make sure the person knows what activities exist to quickly get them involved. In Boulder, I point people to a web post I wrote with several of the high-impact, easy-to-access events (http://startuprev.com/l0).

If someone is visiting from out of town, the leader should quickly introduce the person to about 10 people she thinks are relevant so the visitor can quickly get a bunch of meetings set up to explore the local startup community. Although a leader can occasionally chaperone a person around, it's more powerful to get the community to work by building a culture in which everyone in the community is willing to spend time with someone new in town.

Leaders need to be inclusive of other members of the startup community who want to be leaders. Becoming a leader in a startup community is a function of what you do rather than being voted into office or selected by some secret committee in a dark, smoke-filled room. Leaders should quickly parcel out assignments to any entrepreneur who expresses interest in taking on a leadership role. The best startup community leaders are constantly nurturing new leaders, handing off existing activities to them, and then taking on new responsibilities and starting up new sets of activities.

There will be situations in which someone is fundamentally a bad actor. This person might be a caustic personality, dishonest, emotionally unstable, or simply a bad person. Startup communities behave like an organism that has been invaded when it comes in contact with people like this, and it quickly rejects them. The risk of an occasional organ rejection is worth the risk of being completely inclusive, especially as the scale of the startup community grows.

PLAY A NON-ZERO-SUM GAME

Many people approach business as a zero-sum game: There are winners and losers. This is stupid and counterproductive in the context of a startup community. Startup communities are often a tiny fraction of what they could ultimately become. As a result, there is a huge amount of untapped opportunity. Approaching it as a non-zero-sum game is much more powerful.

For starters, fully embrace the notion of increasing returns. The goal of everyone in the startup community should be to create something that is durable for a very long time. Although ups and downs with individual companies will always happen, view the startup community as a whole entity. If there is more startup activity, this will generate more attention to the startup community, which will generate even more activity.

View the percentage of your local economy that the startup community contributes as its market share. If the macro environment gets better, so will the overall dynamic of the startup community. The macro cycles are unpredictable, but these up-and-down swings will likely only have impact on the overall macro. During downturns, there are actually opportunities for the startup community to gain market share of the local economy.

We've seen this aggressively play out in the most recent economic cycle. Although the global financial downturn that started in 2008 has continued to cast a dark cloud over world economies, startup communities in the United States and throughout the world have been growing significantly during this period. In the past two years, much attention has turned to the power of entrepreneurship to revive the global economy. Against the backdrop of a weak global economy, we regularly see a strong local economy in cities such as Boulder that have a high entrepreneurial density.

The best of these local startup communities aren't playing zero-sum games. The leaders are embracing everyone who wants to engage in startups and are building long-term foundations for continued growth. When a startup fails (which is inevitable for many) the local community quickly absorbs the people involved into other companies because there is almost always a supply/demand imbalance between available employees and available jobs in rapidly growing startup communities. The entrepreneurs aren't shamed when they fail; it's quite the opposite reaction. They immediately are welcomed as advisors for other companies, entrepreneurs in residence for VC firms, and mentors or executives in residence for accelerators like TechStars. Although many take a short break to catch their breath, they often get back in the game quickly. That's what entrepreneurs do.

BE MENTORSHIP DRIVEN

Mentorship, when done correctly, is magical. A great mentor has no expectations of what she is going to get out of the mentor-mentee relationship when she embarks on it. Rather, the mentor is focused on a "give before you get" dynamic, with a willingness to let the relationship go wherever it takes her.

The best leaders can be incredible mentors. They recognize that being a mentor is a key part of the role of a leader and allocate their energy accordingly. Occasionally I'll hear people who declare themselves to be leaders say nonsensical things like "I don't have time to be a mentor." They fundamentally miss the point of what a leader does.

Leaders should be focused on mentorship at several levels. They should be mentoring other leaders, working with anyone who wants to be a leader in the startup community to help them become a leader. They should be mentoring other entrepreneurs, especially those early in their careers who are searching for new mentors. And they should be mentoring each other, because the best mentor-mentee relationships come when the relationship turns into a peer relationship.

Although there isn't a clear amount of time someone should play a mentor role, I love Google's concept of 20 percent time, by which every employee gets to spend 20 percent of their work time on whatever project they want. As a leader, I try to spend 20 percent of my time mentoring entrepreneurs and other leaders—roughly split 50–50 between the two categories. It's not exact, and I'm sure there are stretches during which I end up spending either more or less depending on other things that I've got going on, but over a long period of time I expect my time averages out this way.

I try to keep my mentoring activity unstructured and nonspecific. Instead, I am flexible and responsive to the people I'm mentoring. Some want a specific amount of time each month. Others want to reach out whenever they have a need. Either method works for me.

Most important is the "lead by example" role. In my case, I continually tell people why it's important to be a mentor, but I also show it by being a mentor. Others see my behavior and can learn from it. Part of the power of it, especially in the context of leadership of a startup community, is to show other leaders how to do it, and share the benefits across the whole startup community.

There's no better way to explain this other than from the point of view of one amazing mentor (David Cohen) talking about the behavior of another mentor (Mark Solon) in a real situation they were in. Following is the description, in David's words.

One of the most successful companies I've ever invested in almost disappeared within its first year. As a result of the help of one amazing mentor it is now a large, rapidly growing, and extremely valuable company.

That company is SendGrid, a TechStars company from 2009. SendGrid is now part of the infrastructure of the Internet, having already helped companies successfully deliver tens of billions of transactional e-mails. Mark Solon and I were seed investors in the company and served on the board of directors together. Like many companies that are successful and grow rapidly early in their life, SendGrid had early interest from potential acquirers. The founders of the company planned to build a big business from the very beginning. However, when real money is tossed on the table in front of you, it's easy to be tempted. At one point, the founders decided that it might make sense to sell the company. Mark and I thought that if the company was acquired at this early point, we'd be doing a huge disservice to ourselves and the investors in our funds. But more importantly, we thought we'd be doing a huge disservice to the founders.

Of course, we had no crystal ball. This could have been the best offer that SendGrid would ever get. It was a life-changing financial offer for the founders from a great acquirer. These things make it hard to say no. This is where Mark Solon jumped into action and really shined as a mentor to the founders.

Mark made it clear right away that if the founders decided they wanted to sell, he would not stand in their way. He would support them completely. However, he also made it clear that he'd be very disappointed. I vividly remember Mark telling the founders that "companies like SendGrid don't come along every day." Mark took a very Socratic approach to explore what the founders really wanted. What did they want SendGrid to become? How did they define success? Did they feel that SendGrid would ultimately be worth much more than this offer? Did they think that future financing would be available to them? Did they think that they could be the best in the world at this one thing? Did they think the acquirer could come out with a competitive product in a reasonable time period? Mark also expressed his opinion that other acquirers would come knocking on the door soon enough. Mark's approach clearly put the founders first and because of that the founders correctly viewed Mark as looking out for their best interests and not just his own as a venture capitalist.

The founders decided not to take the early exit. I can't give you the details, but it's now extremely clear that this was a good decision for the founders regardless of what happens next. As with all good mentorship, the key is that the founders ultimately made this decision. Mark acted as a mentor and a friend first, admitted that he could be totally wrong, and let the founders decide.

David Cohen, TechStars, @davidcohen

In addition to David and Mark being awesome mentors, this example shows another powerful dynamic about mentorship—that of mentors learning from each other. Several months after the SendGrid situation resolved, I recall a conversation with David where he explained to me what Mark had done, how he had done it, and what David learned. I've since been in situations in which I've seen David employ similar approaches that he clearly learned from Mark. Mentors never stop teaching, and learning, regardless of the situation.

HAVE POROUS BOUNDARIES

The best startup communities have porous boundaries. It's acceptable for people to flow from one company to another. Leaders talk to each other and share strategies, relationships, ideas, and resources. When someone leaves one company for another, they aren't shunned. When someone moves to town, they are welcomed. When someone leaves town, they are missed, and celebrated every time they come through for a visit.

Although some communities have factions, over time the short-term benefit of the factions are often outweighed by porous boundaries. If you study places like Silicon Valley, you see a continual shift of people from one subset of the community to another, and, for some reason, these subsets have come to be called "mafias." At moments in time you might have a Yahoo! mafia, PayPal mafia, a Google mafia, or a Facebook mafia. Although the members of each mafia share a common set of experiences, they also co-mingle as new companies are created and subsequently acquired by other companies. Although the personal relationships may have short-term complexities, the participants who take a longer view, who embrace their specific mafia, but also encourage and participate in porous boundaries between these mafias, end up playing the best long-term game.

I've seen this in action many times. One of my favorite experiences was in the first year of TechStars in 2007. Two of the mentors had been founders of competing companies. Although each company had long since been acquired, the animosity between these two founders was strong, bordering on hatred. Furthermore, these two entrepreneurs didn't really have a direct relationship; rather, their relationship was through their co-founders, who truly despised each other as a result of a lot of direct conflict when the companies were competing with each other. Given their interests, these two founders ended up mentoring the same company. Within a few weeks they started spending time together and realized they both liked and respected each other. By the end of TechStars, they were good friends and were working on several things together.

GIVE PEOPLE ASSIGNMENTS

People approach me on a daily basis and ask how they can get involved in the Boulder startup community. These requests come in many different forms and with various levels and amounts of background information. It's impossible for me to spend the required time filtering out who is serious and who isn't, so I've come up with a simple approach that I use both in dealing with these offers to get involved and with anyone else who wants to engage with me in something I'm involved with. My approach is to give the person an assignment.

The assignments are straightforward. I try to quickly think of something the person could do that would immediately be helpful. Often the actual assignment is trivial, but it does require that the person do something. These are always assignments that can be completed within an hour, and often within a few minutes, with minimal specific knowledge.

One of three things happens. Half the time I never hear from the person again. I view this as a blessing—the person wasn't serious about helping or engaging and has self-selected out. Occasionally I'll hear from these people again, but usually I never do. When I do hear from them again, I ask them about the assignment, especially if they once again ask to engage in some way. Sometimes they do it, but most of the time they go away again.

A quarter of the time the person does the assignment and reports back. This is useful, because I can now filter this person into the category of "a doer." Every startup community needs people to do things; there are an infinite number of specific tasks that are needed on an ongoing basis. Finding people who are good at just getting stuff done is hard. Once I've found someone like this, I keep giving them more assignments that increase in complexity and ambition on a gradual basis. The great doers just keep on doing.

The remaining situations are magical. People don't just do the assignments, they take them to the next level. They figure out where they can take their assignments, how the assignments fit into a broader context, and make the assignments their own. They do the specific assignments, but they use the assignments as starting points for going a lot further on whatever path I was sending them. These people are leaders, and they quickly take ownership of aspects of the startup community that are interesting to them.

Giving people assignments works as a tool for figuring out who are doers and who are leaders. I use this approach in many different areas of my life in which I initiate projects and provide leadership. This approach is inclusive because I am giving people who want to engage an opportunity, but they have to do something to actually engage. Of course, when they do engage there is a much more significant level of involvement.

EXPERIMENT AND FAIL FAST

The phrase *fail fast* is used throughout the startup ecosystem and has come to encapsulate the notion of continually trying new things, measuring the results, and either modifying the approach or doubling down, depending on the outcome. Eric Ries in his book *The Lean Startup* and the corresponding activity around the lean startup methodology has recently popularized this.

This approach is a key attribute of vibrant startup communities. Think of your startup community as a lean startup—one that needs to try lots of experiments, measure the results, and pivot when things aren't working. It's not that you should fail fast across the entire startup community; instead you should fail fast on specific initiatives that don't go anywhere, attract little interest, or generate no impact.

Within a startup community, there are often grand plans that are defined at the outset of a new set of initiatives. This especially happens when one of the feeders tries to play a leadership role, a broad new program such as Startup Colorado emerges, or we enter an election cycle and the new administration (federal, state, or local) starts a new innovation-related program. Although some of these programs are additive, they often have a long list of objectives to accomplish without any real thought to the weighting or impact of the specific initiatives.

Many of these initiatives don't work or shouldn't work. However, because they've been defined as part of the overall objectives of the initiative, time and energy get spent on them. Months pass and there is very little progress. At the end of a year, there is always some version of a review of the past year. Intellectually honest organizations call out which initiatives had little or no progress; great organizations kill the initiatives that were failing and put their energy behind the ones that are working.

One easy filter is whether leaders for the individual initiatives emerge on their own. If the leaders of the overall organization have to assign the initiatives, then these initiatives likely are of lower value. However, if participants in the organization or the broader startup community step up and take on the specific initiatives, their chance of succeeding is much higher. More importantly, the fact that individuals are drawn to lead specific initiatives emphasizes the relative importance of the initiatives.

Having specific initiatives fail must be an accepted part of the culture of a startup community. As in entrepreneurship, failure is simply part of the process of creating something great, rather than an endpoint. If failure is not acceptable, bad ideas will perpetuate and people who ultimately decide they aren't going to spend more time on something destined to fail will withdraw from the community. To be successful, embrace failure as part of the process.

CHAPTER SIX

CLASSICAL PROBLEMS

As I travel around talking to entrepreneurs about their startup communities, I've heard a consistent set of complaints and have run into similar problems over and over again. Some of these problems are deep rooted and difficult to address in the short term; others require a simple behavior change. In this chapter, I'll discuss a number of these classical problems along with suggestions about what you can do about them.

THE PATRIARCH PROBLEM

The first of the classical problems that stall progress in a startup community is the patriarch problem. In moments of frustration, I call this the old-white-guy problem. At its core, it's one of the key challenges of a hierarchical organizational model, one in which the most powerful people are the ones at the top of the hierarchy. In many cities, especially in the United States, these patriarchs are the old white guys who made their money many years ago but still run the show.

If you observe robust startup communities over a long period of time, they don't exhibit this problem. Silicon Valley is a shining example of this. With each new generation there is a new wave of leaders. Although there are constant debates about whether Silicon Valley is a meritocracy or biased against women and minorities, there is no question that the leaders of yesterday encourage and embrace the leaders of tomorrow, mentor them, and comfortably make room for them in the ecosystem.

I started my first company in Boston when I was 19. I clearly remember feeling like the youngest guy in the room. In my early 20s, we had several customers who embraced us for our youth, whereas others were skeptical of our ability to be serious businesspeople. In one case, we almost lost a large customer when they found out my age because they couldn't believe a CEO of a company could be 21. As I got older, I still felt like the youngest person in the room (and often was), but I became more aware of the structures and constraints of the Boston startup community because of my age. I was typecast as a young, Jewish, MIT software guy. Although that might have been true, I hated that I got a label.

When I moved to Boulder, I realized that none of this existed. The community was much smaller, the hierarchy didn't matter much, and when someone tried to put someone else in a box, they were often rejected or ignored by the system. Sure, there were some who said limiting things like "when I was young it worked this way and you'll have to work your way up as well," but, in general, the community was much flatter, and hierarchies didn't exist.

Interestingly, I did notice the patriarch problem when I engaged with the Denver startup community. It was something that stood out early on; Boulder operated as a network and Denver operated as a hierarchy. In Denver, it mattered who you were, where you went to school, where you had worked, and who you knew. In contrast, the only thing that mattered in Boulder was what you did. When I reflect on the last 16 years that I've lived here, this defines the difference between the Boulder and Denver startup communities, and it is a powerful way to determine whether there is a patriarch problem in your startup community.

When people ask me the solution to the patriarch problem, I offer two answers. First, I suggest that you just have to wait for a bunch of people to die. Although this is harsh, it's often hard to change the behavioral dynamics of people who are stuck in a hierarchical model, and as a result you just have to wait them out.

Next, the leaders of the startup community should simply ignore the patriarchs. Go do your thing without getting the approval of the patriarchs. Lead, and let them come to you if they want. Some will, and when they do they'll love what they see.

COMPLAINING ABOUT CAPITAL

I've been an entrepreneur and investor for the past 27 years. I've lived and invested in Dallas, Boston, and Boulder and have invested in companies in many other cities throughout the United States including Seattle; San Francisco; Los Angeles; San Diego; Chicago; Austin; Portland; Denver; Washington, DC; Atlanta; New York; New Jersey; and some I can't remember. Over and over I hear one thing from entrepreneurs: "There is not enough capital here."

My message is the same for entrepreneurs—let it go. There will always be an imbalance between supply of capital and demand for capital. The whole idea of "enough capital" is nonsensical, and complaining about it doesn't actually impact it.

Many startup communities have specific initiatives to attract more capital to their area. Some of these are government led, such as state funds-of-funds to invest in VC funds that commit to making investments in a specific region. Others are university-sponsored VC funds or university startup grant programs. Although some of these programs are effective and have impact on funding new companies, they don't actually solve the fundamental supply/demand imbalance.

Boulder is a case in point of this. When I moved to Boulder in the mid-1990s, many entrepreneurs complained that there wasn't enough capital here and that was one of the reasons they had difficulty getting funding. In the late 1990s, there were a large number of startups competing for the capital that magically scaled up to meet this much larger number of companies, much to the delight of the local newspapers that regularly ran articles about the increased amount of VC investment in Colorado. At the peak in the early 2000s, a number of new VC firms were created with focused regional fund strategies to invest in Colorado-based companies.

By 2010, many of these VC firms were out of business. Although they made many investments locally over their lifetime, their performances were subpar, and many of their investors (the limited partner community) believed that a regional strategy was ineffective. Granted, many of these firms planted the seeds of their own demise, either by making too many marginal investments or by proclaiming that they were the leaders in the Colorado region, seeing all the great deals, but not realizing that all their peers were saying exactly the same thing, thereby discrediting everyone. Regardless, their funds didn't perform well enough for their investors to continue to invest in them.

Once again, some entrepreneurs are saying that there's not enough capital here. However, the number of new startups, especially in Boulder, is higher than ever before. More importantly, the number of breakaway companies that are growing rapidly and attracting significant amounts of capital from VCs around the country is higher than I've ever seen it. These are real businesses with entrepreneurs who aren't worried about the amount of local capital. Instead, they are focused on creating businesses around a problem they are obsessed about. They believe they can raise the capital they need to scale their business regardless of the local supply of capital. By concentrating on something they can control, they build real companies while having a strong impact on the development of the startup community.

BEING TOO RELIANT ON GOVERNMENT

Although government can play a constructive role in startup communities, a reliance on government to either lead or provide key resources for the effort of building a startup community over a long period of time is a misguided view.

Earlier, I talked about government's role as a feeder. When a startup community starts relying on government to be a leader, bad things happen. First, government often has less money to apply to things than people think it does. As a result, there's often a big mismatch between expectation and reality when it comes time to actually fund something. Next, very few people in government have a background as entrepreneurs, and, as a result, they don't really understand startups in any depth. Consequently the language, the activities, and the interactions are awkward and often ineffective. Government also moves at a much slower pace than entrepreneurs and, when it's in a leadership role, it stifles the individual leadership that emerges. Finally, government runs on a very different time cycle—typically two to four years—than entrepreneurs do.

Think back to the difference between a hierarchy and a network. Government operates as a hierarchy: There are clear roles, chain of command, approval and resource allocation processes, and bureaucracy. In contrast, the best startup communities operate as networks: a broad, loosely affiliated set of leaders and organizations that are working in parallel on a variety of different initiatives. There is rarely a leader of a network, just nodes that are interconnected.

Entrepreneurs live in networks. Government lives in a hierarchy. Although mixing the two isn't fatal, having a network depend on a hierarchy is, as Oliver Williamson (professor at University of California, Berkeley and recipient of the Nobel Prize in Economics) explains in his classic book, *Markets and Hierarchies*.

MAKING SHORT-TERM COMMITMENTS

When I talk to groups of people about startup communities, I begin by asking which of the people in the audience are entrepreneurs. I give a short explanation of how the people with their hands up are the ones who have the potential to be the leaders for the startup community. I then ask them to keep their hands up if they plan to be here 20 years from now. For the ones whose hands are still up, I assert that they are the ones who really can be the leaders.

As I've said earlier, one of the key principles of building a startup community is that it takes a long time. Although I toss around a 20-year number, this is really the minimum. Optimally, it's 20 years from today, and that number resets to another 20 years every day. After you've been at it for a decade, it still requires a 20-year commitment.

The 20-year timeframe signifies a generation to me. It takes a generation of effort to get a startup community up and running in a sustainable way. The first few years of renewal, which many startup communities are going through right now, are exciting, and progress is easy to measure. However, after a few years, the rate of change often slows, macroeconomic dynamics overshadow whatever is going on locally, the political infrastructure changes or simply is less fresh and exciting. This is when the real work happens— day after day, week after week, month after month. Entrepreneurs continue to build their companies, and the ones who have taken on the additional effort of leading the startup community just stay after it.

Although there's nothing wrong with not being committed to a particular geography for the next 20 years, it makes it hard to be a leader. You can have short-term impact, but recognize that, for it to be sustained, you'll need to hand it off to someone else. That's often challenging, especially if the thing you are working on is a multiyear project.

HAVING A BIAS AGAINST NEWCOMERS

A key principle of startup communities that I discussed earlier is the importance of welcoming anyone new who shows up in the community, either temporarily or permanently. Historically, many cities ran as hierarchies and newcomers had to earn their way into the hierarchy. This is dumb, and the exact opposite of what you want to do with a startup community.

In Boulder, when someone new shows up in town, the entrepreneurs swarm them. It doesn't matter if it's someone looking for a job, someone who has previously started a great company, or someone who is well known throughout the entrepreneurial world. Our goal, as a community, is to make the person feel welcome and immediately get integrated into anything they want to be involved in.

If someone sends me an e-mail saying they are coming to Boulder to visit, I immediately introduce them to a bunch of entrepreneurs. I tune these introductions based on the person and their background, looking to introduce them to people who I think they will be most interested in. I've heard regularly that, within an hour, their schedule for the trip is completely full, showing the responsiveness of the Boulder entrepreneurs to anyone coming to visit.

ATTEMPT BY A FEEDER TO CONTROL THE COMMUNITY

In many communities the feeders masquerade as leaders and in some cases try to control what's going on in the startup community. This is a syndrome

I refer to as feeder control, and it stifles short-term growth and long-term health of the startup community.

VCs are some of the worst offenders of this. As I mentioned earlier, VCs are important feeders, but it's very hard for them to be leaders. Although there are exceptions, many VCs, especially in smaller cities or regions that are not as well known for entrepreneurship, position themselves as gatekeepers for people outside the startup community. Phrases similar to "we know all the interesting things going on" or "we see all the best deals" reinforce this position yet are almost always false. This is a classical hierarchical view of the world and simply doesn't work in a widely networked startup community.

Many of the best entrepreneurs are turned off by this type of attitude and consciously avoid engaging with these VCs. More importantly, many VCs sit back and wait for the entrepreneurs to come to them, rather than engaging deeply in whatever is going on around them, regardless of whether they have an investment in a particular company. Either way, this kind of behavior rarely accelerates the growth of a startup community.

Government is another instigator of feeder control. Although this happens at a federal, state, and local level, it's most obvious at a state level. A new governor is elected. After the typical six-month settling-in process, he and the recently appointed head of economic development declare that innovation is a key driver of economic growth for the state and they convene an "innovation council." This innovation council takes another six months to get going while it recruits the appropriate high-profile members. It then creates a set of high-profile public events to spread innovation across the state. Everything is abstract, filled with pomp and circumstance, and usually disconnected with whatever is actually going on in the startup community. Many people involved use it as a way to generate more visibility for their company, their cause, or their agenda and very little work actually gets done. Before you know it, it's time for another election cycle and the initiatives fade into the background as the governor focuses on getting elected again.

Another example is the university that tries to position itself in the middle of all the startup activity in a community. Although universities are great feeders, their biggest value to a startup community is often a steady stream of new young, smart people with a secondary value of lots of space for convening events. In a few cases, like MIT and Stanford, there is a tremendous culture of entrepreneurship among professors and students, which often generates lots of new startups, but this is the exception. When universities try to emulate MIT and Stanford, they often try to position themselves at the center of all the entrepreneurial activity, viewing their role through the lens of technology transfer (we must generate lots of new startups) or control over the innovation (all the IP belongs to us—we will share it if we get a piece of it). Neither of these approaches are particularly effective.

Although each of these types of feeders, and others, are important, when they try to control what's going on in the startup community, they often retard the actual growth of the startup community. You'll notice that some of the feeders, such as governments and universities, run on a strong hierarchy model. When a hierarchy instead of a network drives an entity, it almost always classifies it as a feeder. A natural force within hierarchies is top-down control over all activities; use this as a warning sign that feeder control is in the mix.

CREATING ARTIFICIAL GEOGRAPHIC BOUNDARIES

Entrepreneurship doesn't follow geographic boundaries. It's one of the key reasons entrepreneurship is so powerful in the United States—city and state boundaries are defined for political convenience and generally don't impact the flow of people or companies across local geographies.

Let's use the Boston startup community as an example. What is commonly known as the Boston startup community consists of several cities including Boston, Cambridge, Waltham (Rte. 128), and Hopkinton (Rte. 495). Historically when people talked about Boston, they talked about Rte. 128, which even has a sign on it that says "America's Technology Highway." Today, however, much of the startup activity is in Cambridge and near downtown Boston.

Even within Cambridge, however, you have different neighborhoods (Kendall Square, Central Square, Harvard Square) and within Boston you have different neighborhoods (Innovation District, Leather District, South End). Although these neighborhoods are a walk or a short train ride apart, they have distinct superlocal characteristics that all contribute to the local characteristics of Boston.

However, what prevents a Boston-based company from expanding to another city or picking up and moving to the Bay Area, like the famous examples of Facebook and Dropbox? Nothing! And that's the beauty of it—this permeability of boundaries requires each community to continue to improve if it wants to keep the best companies local.

This applies to movement within cities. One of Boulder's weaknesses, which I'll discuss later, is lack of office space. Once a company reaches about 100 people, it becomes very hard for it to stay in downtown Boulder. Many of these companies move to the outskirts of Boulder, but once they hit several hundred people, they once again run out of space and often move to one of the neighboring cities like Broomfield. Although the startup communities are connected, these startup neighborhoods proliferate.

As a result, high-growth startups aren't constrained by city or state borders. When they hit a national border and expand into another country, lots of issues suddenly appear. Immigration, business law, employment law, and tax rules are obvious ones, but there are many more subtle ones, including culture, societal view of entrepreneurship, and views about success and failure. So at a country level, geographic borders matter a lot, but at a state and city level, they don't matter much at all.

PLAYING A ZERO-SUM GAME

Once members of the startup community realize that geographic borders are artificial, they often fall into the trap of playing a zero-sum game, where they win at the expense of the neighboring startup community. "Our community is better than yours" starts popping up. Government initiatives to recruit startups from other states appear. Major branding initiatives around demonstrating that "we are the best startup community" emerge. Resistance appears when there is an opportunity to collaborate across geographies.

This is dumb. As a society, we are far from the saturation point in terms of entrepreneurship. Although there is not an infinite capacity for it, playing a zero-sum game, especially within neighboring geographies, simply stifles the growth of the startup ecosystem. Instead, take a network approach and connect your startup community with neighboring ones.

This is the approach we have taken with Startup Colorado. The north-south highway connecting the state is I-25. There are four major cities within two hours of each other—from north to south we have Fort Collins, Boulder, Denver, and Colorado Springs. Although Boulder is the smallest, it has the most robust startup community. Yet each of the other three cities has incredible inherent resources for entrepreneurship, many of which are different from but complementary to those in Boulder. In the first year of Startup Colorado, one of our initiatives was to export some of the activities in Boulder to the surrounding cities. These started with regularly repeating events such as the Boulder Denver New Tech Meetup (the second largest monthly meetup in the United States, now topping 500 people at each monthly event) as well as biweekly Open Coffee Clubs (a movement that was started in London by Saul Klein and has spread throughout the world), Office Hours (where experienced entrepreneurs will meet with anyone), and Startup Weekends (a 54-hour simulation of entrepreneurship).

Although these activities may seem straightforward, that's by design. The goal is to get the leaders in the other cities to take a networked, bottom-up approach to getting people actively engaged in the startup community. The leaders in the Boulder startup community didn't view things as a zero-sum game, and instead of telling entrepreneurs throughout the state to move to Boulder, they exported things that were working for them to the neighboring communities.

HAVING A CULTURE OF RISK AVERSION

A local culture of risk aversion is another classical inhibitor of startup communities. As I travel around the United States, I often hear from people that they are afraid of investing time in their startup community because they are afraid there won't be a payoff. This generally comes in two forms: (1) a concern about investing your time in something that doesn't have impact, and (2) fear of rejection by other leaders in the startup community.

In the first case, I encourage people to take more chances but give their effort time boundaries. Great entrepreneurs try lots of things that don't end up working. If you have an idea or initiative that is interesting to you, just get started. If, after a few months, it isn't going anywhere, you've lost interest in it, or you're having trouble getting others to engage, take that as a signal that the initiative isn't working in its current form. You then have two choices: change it or kill it. In either case, you are moving on to the next iteration of the idea. Rather than being concerned about wasting your time, make sure you learn something from what didn't work.

In the case of fear of rejection by other leaders in the startup community, let it go. The more people in the startup community who step up and try things, the more the startup community will be open to people trying things. If you have a patriarch problem in your community, just ignore the existing hierarchy. If your initiative doesn't work, try another one. Build a reputation for trying stuff, collecting data, pivoting, and improving. Over time, that's much more attractive and impactful than a reputation of being afraid to give it a shot. And it's much better for the long-term health of the startup community.

AVOIDING PEOPLE BECAUSE OF PAST FAILURES

I was recently in Iceland for the inaugural Startup Iceland event. Although I had no specific reason to go, my wife, Amy, and I had never been to Iceland

and we figured it would be fun to go hang out, see Reykjavik, and meet a bunch of entrepreneurs. We had an awesome time, saw a fascinating country, and met a community of people energized around entrepreneurship, partially as a result of the spectacular economic collapse that Iceland recently had, which caused many people to hit reset and start over.

I remember one of the entrepreneurs distinctly. He was sharp, smart, and had clearly been through a lot. I heard about his previous success and failure, but spent most of my time talking with him about what he was currently working on. He was somewhat cynical about the Startup Iceland activity, but he was engaged because, at his core, he was an entrepreneur and attracted to other entrepreneurs. However, I sensed something was off.

I asked one of the Startup Iceland leaders what the story was with the entrepreneur in question. The response was simple, but enlightening: "He burned a lot of bridges when his last startup failed—a lot of people don't want to work with him." I asked if he had done anything illegal or just failed. "He just failed and made a mess, but he wasn't graceful about it." I pressed on what *graceful* meant and didn't really get a good answer, but it was clear that our failed entrepreneur had tarnished his reputation and was being avoided because of his failure.

I encouraged my new friend to let this go and embrace the failed entrepreneur. I asserted that he'd learned an enormous amount from his failure. More importantly I suggested that by embracing the failed entrepreneur, it would encourage more entrepreneurs to take more risks. It would shift the culture around failure in a positive way.

CHAPTER SEVEN

ACTIVITIES AND EVENTS

U p to this point I've been giving you a framework and talking in abstractions about how to create a great startup community. In this chapter, we shift to some specific examples of things various leaders in Boulder took on, got going, and turned into fundamental components of our startup community. The impact of each one varies, and individually you might not view any of them as a particularly huge endeavor, but collectively they provide a powerful base that our startup community is built on.

In each section, I'll provide a brief introduction, and then you can read, in the leader's words, about how the initiative came about. The initiatives are roughly in the order they were created, to give you a sense of how they build on each other while being individually created and led.

YOUNG ENTREPRENEURS ORGANIZATION

When I first moved to Boulder in 1995, the only person I knew was Verne Harnish. Verne was the founder of the Young Entrepreneurs Organization

(YEO) (http://startuprev.com/d0), which he'd started in the late 1980s. YEO was a membership-based organization for entrepreneurs of companies under the age of 40 (now 50) who had founded companies with over $1 million in annual revenue.

I joined YEO in 1990 after attending the first Birthing of Giants event, which was sponsored by YEO, *Inc.* magazine, and MIT Enterprise Forum. That first class included a number of amazing people, including Ted Leonsis, whose company was acquired by AOL after which Ted went on to become the vice chairman of AOL, and Alan Trefler, whose company Pegasystems (NASDAQ: PEGA) went public a few years later. I was one of the youngest participants, and my company, Feld Technologies, barely crested the $1 million mark.

Shortly after this first Birthing of Giants event, I started the Boston YEO chapter. I'm still friendly with many of the entrepreneurs who formed the initial core group of YEO Boston, along with many of the entrepreneurs I met at YEO International conferences. Through YEO, I had found my peer group and realized how critically important it was, at an early point in my career, to spend time with one's peers.

Shortly after I moved to Boulder, I started looking for other entrepreneurs like me. Boulder didn't have a YEO chapter, so I asked a lawyer and an accountant who I had met to reach out to all the entrepreneurs they knew who might fit the criteria for YEO. The first meeting, held at The Boulderado Hotel, included Tim Enwall. Following, in Tim's words, is the story of the formation of YEO Boulder, which has expanded to become EO Colorado (http://startuprev.com/j1), and it is still going strong today.

While the earliest days of the Boulder startup community were highlighted by the extraordinary success of Jesse Aweida and Juan Rodriguez at StorageTek and subsequent storage-related startups funded by them and Hill, Carmen, and Washing, the beginnings of a more communal effort among startup execs began in the mid-90s when the Young Entrepreneur's Organization (YEO) chapter was founded in Colorado and the first "forum" (a group of 10 or so founder/CEOs who supported each other) was instantiated in Boulder.

Criteria to join YEO were simple: members had to be founders of a company with more than $1 million in annual revenue and be under the age of 40. The purpose of YEO is to provide tangible peer support to founders building high-growth, successful companies both through education on relevant topics and through small peer-support groups ("forums") consisting of up to a dozen people. Each forum member gets to know his other forum members intimately because of the rules related to participation and contribution, as well as the candid nature of the dialogue. Members are taught that the more honest they are with their challenges and opportunities, the more they will get out of the experience. Members of forums often—as is true of Forum 1 in Boulder—stay connected to each other for the rest of their lives. The early spirit of founder sharing candidly and generously was born in Forum 1.

This sharing spirit quickly spread from within the forum members to outside the forum. New, young high-growth founders were quickly welcomed into the community through the informal network—coffees, breakfasts, YEO events, and other events typically hosted by local service providers like legal and accounting firms. One knew that, if one had a challenge, a new experience, an opportunity to potentially pursue, then help, and often multiple helping hands, was close at hand. Because the network was tight and within easy coffee or breakfast distance, it flourished. Because members received as often as they gave, a very natural sharing community evolved.

Even today, members of this network bring new members to the network, providing encouragement and support. Many of them are mentors in the TechStars program and are quick to offer their contributions or services to other entrepreneurial activities in the community. Each frequently provides support to the other with their next startup or a difficult problem. This ethos of sharing and support that began within the 10-member Forum 1 has extended into fairly far-flung efforts including cross participation in philanthropic efforts important to each of them.

Ultimately, it is this ethos of unequivocal sharing—desiring absolutely nothing in return for one's contribution, one's experiences—that has created the nucleus around which others can't help but contribute in the same fashion. It is now simply expected.

—*Tim Enwall, Tendril*

These early Boulder YEO members, including Tim, Paul Berberian, Jared Polis, Ryan Martens, and Jim Lejeal show up regularly today as leaders of the Boulder startup community. In 1996, I once again found my peer group, and 16 years later these entrepreneurs are still providing leadership for the community that I'm part of.

YEO, now called Entrepreneurs Organization (EO) can be found in virtually every city around the world. It's a core part of the entrepreneurial substrate and an inspiration for many of the ideas around startup community that have developed over the years.

OFFICE HOURS

In the late 1990s I became overwhelmed with the number of people who wanted to meet with me. I'd become visible in the Boulder community, both as an entrepreneur and VC investor. Although many people wanted to meet purely for networking purposes, others had specific agendas for getting together.

At some point I realized I had a choice: I could either spend all my time meeting with random people who wanted to get together with me or I could become much less accessible. Neither of these appealed to me, so I created the concept of random days.

One day a month, I'd declare a random day. On this day, I'd spend 15 minutes with anyone. As the steady stream of requests to get together for a coffee or a meal along with the endless referrals from people I knew to "meet with their friend" came in, I'd simply invite them to a 15-minute meeting on random day. When random day came along, I sat in a conference room and had up to 20 short meetings like this before I wore out, called it a day, and went and had a beer.

I've made many great connections on my random days. Numerous people I met now work for companies in which I'm an investor. I've made long-lasting friendships with people in large companies to which I didn't expect I'd have access. Startups, such as TechStars, came out of a random day meeting, and I've learned about a number of curious, unexpected things.

Over time, someone realized this notion of random days was similar to the academic construct of office hours during which a professor makes himself available for a few hours once a week to any student who wants to meet with him. I started referring to random days as office hours, and other members of the startup community, including my partners at Foundry Group, David Cohen, VCs like Kirk Holland and Mark Solon, and lawyers such as Mike Platt and Jason Haislmaier started having office hours on a regular basis.

Other entrepreneurs, such as Niel Robertson, took the concept of office hours and made them their own. In Niel's case, you can often find him having breakfast at Jill's Restaurant from 8 to 9 A.M. when he's in town. Sometimes he dines alone; other times he eats with someone who has reached out to him to get together. Either way, along with the other practitioners of office hours, he makes himself easily accessible to other members of the startup community.

BOULDER DENVER NEW TECH MEETUP

Over the past five years, the Boulder Denver New Tech Meetup has become a local institution. Conceived and led by Robert Reich, it has grown from a modest start to regular events of 500 people, making it the second largest known Tech Meetup in the United States, behind New York. The Boulder event is held at the CU Law Courtroom, one of the largest auditoriums on campus, and it is an example of how CU Law supports the Boulder startup community. Following, in Robert's words, is the story of the Boulder Denver New Tech Meetup.

The first Boulder Denver New Tech (BDNT) was held on August 8, 2006. It was held at the Me.dium offices (a company I had co-founded) and 39 people attended. We promoted the event through word of mouth. Today, almost six years later, the group has 8,000 members and is growing faster than when it first launched.

The basic format has not changed since the original event. Five presenters get five minutes to pitch their new technology followed by five minutes of Q&A. The original format was created at the New York Tech Meetup, but we refined it for Boulder and made it our own.

Our guiding principles for the event are to keep it real and keep it moving. This means if a presenter is not getting to the point, they are nudged along or even cut off. If they are talking at the audience, selling too hard, or presenting something that seems unrealistic, it will be questioned publicly. On the flip side, if they are delivering something the audience is really engaged in understanding, they will get a little extra time.

The first year was focused around recruiting presenters, spreading the word about what was going on in town, and providing a place to break bread and have a beer with friends. Over time, this evolved, but by focusing on these three things, we built a strong foundation in the first 12 Meetups.

By the end of 2007, BDNT had outgrown the Me.dium offices. I looked around Boulder and could not locate a facility that was affordable and that would support 200 people. Coffee shops or offices are awesome when you're under 100 people, but as soon as you grow beyond this amount, the logistics, cost, and crowd dynamics change. Boulder fortunately has a university a half-mile from downtown, so I met with different groups to see if I could find a new home for BDNT. I talked to a number of folks but immediately connected with Brad Bernthal and Phil Weiser from Silicon Flatirons, a group that was within the Law School at the CU Boulder that included supporting entrepreneurship in its charter. A great connection was made early on in BDNT's life, and helping CU Boulder become a world-class institution for entrepreneurs became part of BDNT's mission.

During the same time period, TechStars was seeing its own success, and the Boulder startup scene was growing and attracting more entrepreneurs. BDNT became part of the fabric of this growing startup community and was commonly referenced as the great entrepreneurship event that happens on the first Tuesday of each month.

BDNT was looking for a way to help the community collaborate and embraced Twitter early on. We cobbled together a solution that allowed us to refresh the #BDNT hashtag against the Twitter search engine. This created a real-time commenting system that was displayed on two large monitors during the entire event. In the beginning, it was novel, and it gave the audience a voice. Eventually it became disruptive. We resisted changing it, because we did not want to squash the valuable conversation that was occurring.

During this period we were making the Twitter trending terms list during each event, which helped spread the word. Ultimately we took the live feed down during the presenter talks, increased the refresh rate, and only displayed the Twitter feed during the Q&A. This worked, and we learned an important lesson: a small amount of structure could be used to help guide the event's flow without disrupting the culture. We tried fancy Twitter walls and other services, but in the end, the simplicity of our hacked solution worked and is still used today.

Toward the end of year two, the community was growing at a steady pace and was asking for more specific events like a Ruby on Rails Meetup or a JavaScript Meetup. Instead of trying to create and manage an events business, we added an announcement section to the beginning of the event. Anyone could promote any tech-related event.

We were also getting regular requests for nametags. Surprisingly, the event still felt intimate, even though it was 40 percent new and averaged 250 people per month. We opted to try something different and went for chaos over formality. At the beginning of BDNT, the seated audience was asked to take one minute to meet someone new. The room erupted into a roar and it often took five minutes to quiet everyone down and start the show. Today each event begins using this icebreaker technique.

Not all things that we've tried have been successful. In the peak of the recession, we decided it would be great to help people get jobs. We gave anyone looking for a job the opportunity to stand up and announce what they were looking for and their skills. Way too many people stood up, and it was the most depressing event ever hosted. We never did it again, but we have a resume table and always request people post job opportunities on the free message board. We also tried to facilitate after-meeting sessions, but it never took off. Nonetheless, experimentation and creativity have always been at the heart of BDNT and we are willing to fail fast if something isn't working.

BDNT was at capacity every month for over three years and something had to be done to manage the growth. One of the early goals was to keep the event free, and one-third of the attendees were now coming from the Denver area. Also, the Boulder startup scene began to create more jobs than it could fill each month. Denver was a much larger city only 30 minutes away, so we decided to create a second event. We hoped to replicate a partnership like the one with Silicon Flatirons, but that proved harder to find, and we quickly learned that Denver was a very different animal than Boulder.

The Denver community was more reserved, more geographically spread out than Boulder, and the audience fluctuated between 125 and 500 people. We talked to different schools and ultimately created a partnership with Metro State. They were great hosts, but we were never able to engage the students or the faculty and the facilities were far from intimate. We tried different types of presentations to engage the community and, while most did okay, the one that made a big difference and turned the Denver event around was a nonprofit night.

The community was invited to help different local nonprofits solve technical and business problems that only geeks know how to solve. The event was an amazing success and remains one of the best events hosted each year in Boulder and Denver.

Knowing we could attract the people and get them engaged inspired us to find a solution. We tried a different facility on campus, but ultimately the rules and regulations were just too much to deal with. We decided to find a new space, one that was more intimate and had no issues with alcohol. The Denver BDNT has been at capacity every month since we moved to the MapQuest offices. The people, the space, and free drinks are the key building blocks to getting a tech event off the ground.

When BDNT reached 5,000 members, the community started to change. Many of the entrepreneurs who regularly showed up in the early days were now traveling on a regular basis as they grew their businesses and only showed up intermittently. This freed up space for people interested in tech or entrepreneurship to join the group. The new people were also interested in being inspired and entertained. Getting presenters became challenging, and many of them were first-time entrepreneurs who had never presented in front of a large audience. The community started getting frustrated at the quality of the presentations, so several of us sat down over lunch and discussed a mentoring program that would be a great way to build lasting ties in the community and increase the overall quality of the presentations and the event. It worked.

We created a mentorship program for the new presenters. We gave the mentors veto rights on whether or not a company was ready to present. Month after month experienced presenters were helping less experienced ones, and the quality of the presentations went way up. We continued to tune the model and now hold a group mentoring session one week before the monthly event.

To entertain the crowd, BDNT has used DJs and appcessories like Rock Band, had fireside chats with tech celebrities, hosted office minutes with VCs, and even created fictitious presentations for April Fool's Day. A few of my favorite presentation alternatives we used when we could not get enough presenters included: New Tech Gadgets, where we focused on cool hardware; Under the Microscope, which launched a company at BDNT and for three consecutive months turned the five-minute presentation into a public board meeting; and Micro Failures, where successful entrepreneurs in the community discussed important lessons learned.

Each year we help the community meet the different companies going through TechStars, Founders Institute, the Unreasonable Institute, the Startup Class at Boulder Digital Works, and the CU New Venture Challenge. We try to video as many of the presentations as possible and post them on our Facebook page. Occasionally we even live stream the events.

BDNT has succeeded for the same reasons most startups succeed: a stubborn founder with a vision, an ability to creatively adapt to market demand, and free beer.

—Robert Reich, @menro

When BDNT started, I tried to go every time I was in town. I still go to BDNT a few times a year and continue to be amazed by the energy and enthusiasm in the room, along with the significant number of first-time attendees at each meeting. Whenever someone new comes to Boulder and asks how to plug into the startup community, I suggest they go to BDNT every month, for six months in a row. By the sixth month, they'll become regulars. As far as I know, this has worked every time.

BOULDER OPEN COFFEE CLUB

When Jason Mendelson, one of my partners at Foundry Group, moved to Boulder in 2006, he asked me if there was anything obvious he could do to more quickly get plugged into the local startup scene. I suggested he start an Open Coffee Club. I'd heard about Open Coffee Clubs a few months ear-lier from Saul Klein of Index Partners who had started the first one in Lon-don. Jason did a little research on how Saul was doing it, and the result was something pretty awesome. Following is Jason's story of how the Boulder Open Coffee Club came about.

One activity that helps foster a startup community is a regularly occurring event by the community for community. This is the oppo-site of large events or special award ceremonies; it's a small gathering that isn't special but happens on a regular basis where members of the community interact deeply with one another in an informal setting. Boulder Open Coffee Club is an example of this type of event that we've had great success with.

We did not invent the idea of the Open Coffee Club; rather, we got the idea from Saul Klein, who started the first Open Coffee Club in London (http://startuprev.com/b1). We heard about it and decided that we'd try an experiment in Boulder to see if we could generate interest in folks getting around a table and hanging out.

We started very simply. We decided that the club needed to be before work (8 A.M. to 9ish), on a regular schedule (every other Tuesday) and at a local coffee shop.

We didn't ask for permission. We posted flyers (this was prior to Twitter's becoming ubiquitous) and blogged about the concept. We positioned it as an "un-meeting" where entrepreneurs and others who were interested in startups could come, hang out, network, and share some stories. We also made it clear that this was going to be a regular event, so that people who couldn't make it would still keep it on their radar.

The first event had nine people show up: seven entrepre-neurs, one venture capitalist (me), and a marketing consultant.

I dominated the first meeting as I was in sell mode for the concept and had an agenda that included current events affecting start-ups, some new products that had recently come on the market, and several updates on local fundraisings. The most important part, however, was asking the attendees what they wanted to get out of the future meetings.

The answers ranged from wanting to trade war stories in a safe environment, to networking, to recruiting, to figuring out how to fundraise, to just hanging out. Looking back, one of the critical roles that I played was putting the energy behind each Boulder Open Coffee Club meeting to make it an informative and entertaining event from the start, even though I didn't know where it would lead. Most importantly, I knew long term that community needed to own this event, not me.

A few months later, 9 people turned into 20, which quickly turned into 40 and necessitated a larger coffee shop. Everyone who showed up at an event was engaged, and regulars started to provide leadership for the newcomers. A typical format evolved and looked something like the following:

- 8 A.M.: Hello and greetings
- 8:05: Current Events—things in the news that were note-worthy. This could be anything from new product launches to new laws and policies that affect startups, to new developer toolkit releases, to ideas on best practices for X, where X could be almost anything. This was usually led by whoever was leading the group.
- 8:30: Open Floor. This was where people could present or ask questions of the group. This included everything from questions about one's particular startups to general questions.

Sometimes people would pitch the group with slides to get feedback before going to present to investors. Many times people would be looking to hire someone and someone across the room was able to help. This was also the part where I stayed out of the fray as much as possible and let the community run the agenda. As the group matured, not all the questions revolved around startups or technology, as the group began to trust each other for all sorts of recommendations. Fun and unexpected connections got made, like my finding a keyboard player for my band at one of the Boulder Open Coffee Club meetings.

- 9:00: Networking. In Boulder the parking meters start charging at 9 A.M., so we figured that people would want to get on with their day, but this is when many people stayed around and networked and followed up with each other from past meetings.

By the end of the first year, I was still going to every event, but several entrepreneurs started taking more of a leadership role and coming up with topics. This was where I knew the inflection point had occurred and the community took over the ownership of the Boulder Open Coffee Club.

Today, the Boulder Open Coffee Club is one of the most vibrant organizations in Boulder. Although the meetings start at 8 A.M., most people arrive at 7:30 A.M. to get a seat, and every meeting is packed with 70 people, which is the maximum our largest local coffee shop can hold. Although we've thought about moving to a larger location, we decided the intimacy of the space, plus the idea that it happens every two weeks and that even if you miss one, you can make the next, was the correct approach. The meeting is now

100 percent run by the community, with several leaders eager to act as moderator—a role that is organically spread around over time.

The impact to the community has been large. Anyone who moves to the area knows how to get plugged in immediately—it's the most frequent and open discussion group in the area. Think of the Boulder Open Coffee Club as Boulder's entrepreneurial Ellis Island. Many companies have been formed and many people hired by startups from people meeting at the Boulder Open Coffee Club. Finally, the knowledge transfer that has occurred within the community has been incredible and accelerated many companies while helping them avoid common mistakes.

As a bonus, it's a blast to get together every other week with good friends who love startups over the best coffee in town, which of course is Atlas Purveyors, should you be in Boulder.

—Jason Mendelson, Foundry Group, @jasonmendelson

The Boulder Open Coffee Club (http://startuprev.com/n1) is still going strong, and a dynamite group of entrepreneurs can be found discussing a wide range of topics at Atlas Purveyors (http://startuprev.com/d1) every other Tuesday. If you are ever in Boulder on a Tuesday morning when Boulder Open Coffee Club is meeting, stop by and pay us a visit.

STARTUP WEEKEND

Startup Weekend was born in Boulder in July 2007. At the time, Andrew Hyde was hanging around and helping out TechStars. He was inspired by the activity around the first TechStars Boulder program and decided to get a gang together to see what it would be like to create a startup in a weekend.

Over 70 people gathered on Friday night to meet each other and brainstorm ideas. There were about 40 different projects, which quickly got narrowed down to 5 that were voted on. The most popular was VoSnap, a simple mobile polling app that became the basis for all the work over the next 48 hours.

Seth Levine, another of my Foundry Group partners, and I provided the food, which included pizza, beer, soda, pretzels, bagels, and a bunch of chocolate stuff. Although I didn't stay the entire weekend, I met a number of new entrepreneurial friends, many whom were working for other startups at the time. We all found Startup Weekend to be a great way to experience the process of a startup while meeting a bunch of peers.

Andrew ran about 80 Startup Weekends around the world before selling Startup Weekend to Marc Nager and Clint Nelsen in 2009, who were quickly joined by a third partner, Franck Nouyrigat. Marc, Clint, and Franck turned Startup Weekend into a 501c(3); got a bunch of smart people involved as advisors, such as David Cohen; expanded rapidly; got a grant from the Kauffman Foundation; and are doing hundreds of Startup Weekends a year around the world.

Following is a current description of how a Startup Weekend works, in Marc's words:

As we all know, there is no better way to learn how to do something than actually doing it; furthermore, there is no better way to improve at something than by practicing. When it comes to starting a company, Startup Weekend is one of the best ways to experience and simulate actually starting a company and being an entrepreneur.

Startup Weekends generally begin on a Friday evening with around 100 developers, designers, businesspeople, government officials, investors, educators, inventors, lawyers, local veterans, students, etc. The average age is around 32 years old, with 9.5 years' work experience, and typically on their third self-proclaimed startup project. After some fun icebreakers, networking, drinks, and likely an off-the-wall or inspirational speaker, the microphone opens to everyone in the room. Each person has their 60-second opportunity to identify what problem they are passionate about solving and their possible solution. On average, about a third of the room will actually pitch an idea.

Following the pitches, everyone is given about an hour to dive in deeper, evaluate, and refine their favorite ideas presented. Utilizing a highly sophisticated voting method of Post-it notes, the top 15 or so ideas bubble to the top and the rest are eliminated. The balance of the first evening is then spent on team formation, which is the most crucial part of the entire weekend.

The top ideas serve as a vehicle for a much more important element—connecting people with similar interests and passions who want to solve the same problem. Learning how to build effective teams is perhaps the most important factor in the ultimate success or failure of a startup.

With teams formed Friday night, everyone embarks on a journey to further define the problem they are addressing and validate the possible solutions they have thought of. Throughout the rest of the weekend, accomplished and experienced entrepreneurs are brought in to act as coaches to help guide teams, teach methodologies, troubleshoot products, ask probing questions, and challenge assumptions. Gallons of coffee and tasty meals are provided to keep teams focused and working hard.

On Sunday evening, teams wrap up what they've learned and present this and their prototypes to the rest of the room. There is a judging panel of local successful entrepreneurs who choose the winners in several different categories. We wrap up Startup Weekend with an after-party where everyone decompresses, shares war stories, dreams of future success, and celebrates their accomplishments with their newfound friends.

—Marc Nager, Startup Weekend, @MarcNager

In 2011 when Marc and team created a formal board of directors for Startup Weekend (http://startuprev.com/d2) I happily agreed to be part of it. Startup Weekend continues to be an amazing way for someone to experience the dynamics of starting a company with a number of other like-minded people over a 54-hour period.

IGNITE BOULDER

There is nothing particularly interesting or remarkable about delivering a PowerPoint presentation. It's a fundamental business skill that most professionals develop during their careers, alongside plugging data into a spreadsheet, sending a thank-you note, and buying donuts for the team.

However, what if you freed the presentation from its office shackles and let it watch zombie movies, indulge its pop-culture vices, and transform itself into a fast-paced jolt of pure human expression? The Ignite series of events, founded in Seattle in 2006, took the staid PowerPoint slideshow format and affixed a rocket to it.

The Ignite format of public speaking is simple. Each speaker gets 20 slides to get their point across, and those slides automatically advance every 15 seconds. The result is an evening of five-minute blasts of perspective, imagination, creativity, hilarity, and pure genius.

Andrew Hyde, Ef Rodriguez, and a few others brought Ignite to Boulder in 2008. Following, in Ef's words, is how it came about.

The first Ignite Boulder was held in a classroom on the University of Colorado at Boulder campus in October 2008, hosted by entrepreneur and author, Andrew Hyde. Over the course of the next four years and almost 20 events, Ignite Boulder grew into a staple of the startup community, emblematic of Boulder's creative, innovative population.

Ignite Boulder is held together by a small band of volunteer organizers, nearly all of whom have spoken at the event. I was lucky enough to speak at one of the earliest editions, coming on board as an organizer shortly afterward and guiding the event as its benevolent dictator until recently.

I want to stress that this isn't my job. No one involved with Ignite Boulder makes any money from it. We take time outside of work to shape the event for free and give the proceeds from ticket sales to local worthy causes. The community is bigger than any venue can hold, so we help out other sectors as often as we can.

Over time, we've added a subgroup of volunteers to help us on the night of each event. The community's ardent support of Ignite Boulder made it obvious that there were dozens of people who wanted to be part of it, if only to work the check-in tables or help distribute posters. I've never seen so many smiles.

Ignite Boulder distinguished itself from other cities' iterations by being exponentially more creative. We believe that if an event is anchored by quality content, it's allowed to be a spectacle. To that end, my team has employed all sorts of nonsense to make the event as spectacular as possible—things like cardboard dinosaur cutouts, inflatable penguins, and cheap bowling trophies given to audience members at random. All of these shenanigans are designed to make Ignite Boulder more than just a night of PowerPoint slides.

We agonize over speaker selection, endeavoring to deliver an evening of social value and originality for an audience of more than 1,400 people. We reject applicants who only want to spam the audience with a disguised sales pitch. Early on, each organizer learns how to unmask a community leech and eject them from consideration. Over time, we got fewer and fewer of those as the event's self-expression agenda has become clear.

The early Ignite Boulder events played to our strengths— general geekery and startup chutzpah. As the event matured and we began to fill the largest venues in town, the subject matter broadened to include a wide variety of topics, attracting speakers with very specialized interests who only wanted to share them with an open-minded audience.

A librarian. A firefighter. A skydiver. A woman who dislikes pandas immensely. Each presentation was a surprise. The audience never knew what was coming next, and if someone wasn't interested in a particular speaker, we were quickly on to the next one within five minutes.

From its inception, the Ignite concept served as a means for community members to speak a little louder, a little faster, in front of a few more people, about something they cared a lot about. Eventually Ignite Boulder's organizers started to ponder the role of Ignite in the broader context of Boulder's startup community. Do we allow truly passionate speakers that aren't necessarily interested in technology, or do we apply an editorial filter to the content that would preserve its nerdy origins?

We concluded that broadening the content was much more interesting. As Ignite grew bigger, we moved to larger venues. As the speakers became more varied, we egged them on with foam fingers. As the community expanded and changed, so did Ignite Boulder.

As a result of our earnest appreciation of new perspectives, the event drew even more people into the community and, in effect, strengthened the bonds that hold it together. Although the event is still rooted in tech and startup culture, we eagerly roll out the red carpet to all of Boulder and continue to evolve Ignite Boulder with every event.

—Ef Rodriguez, @pug

In May 2012, the 18th Ignite Boulder (http://startuprev.com/l2) was held. It was Ef's last, as he's moved to Amsterdam, but he'll be back, at least in spirit, for Ignite 19.

BOULDER BETA

Great startup communities are inclusive—anyone can take initiative and create something new. Tim Falls exemplifies this, as you'll see from his story about the creation of Boulder Beta (http://startuprev.com/d3).

When I moved from Bloomington, Indiana, to Boulder four years ago, I quickly realized I didn't need go far or wait long to find a gathering of startup enthusiasts. The options were endless: walk down Pearl Street Mall any given day, attend one of the focused Meetups held weekly, get caffeinated with fellow techies at Boulder Open Coffee Club every other Tuesday morning, check out the freshest startups at the Boulder Denver New Tech Meetup on CU's campus each month, enjoy a geeky chuckle at Ignite Boulder each quarter, meet the newest batch of TechStars during the summer, or hang out each spring for a week for the startup festival known as Boulder Startup Week.

Upon a bit of self-reflection, I realized how much my peers had done for me since welcoming me to Boulder four years earlier. I went from knowing no one to knowing everyone, in a matter of months. I could call on the pillars of the Boulder tech community to help me with any request; and believe me, I requested. I felt a need to give back. I wanted to play a significant role in sustaining Boulder's awesomeness and taking our community to the next level.

So, I asked myself, "What does the Boulder startup community need that it doesn't currently have?" I recently discovered an event called SF Beta (http://startuprev.com/o0)—a gathering of the coolest young companies and smartest community members of Silicon Valley. The event created a fun, social environment that fosters rich interaction among entrepreneurs, investors, students, and curious minds, in an informal, social environment. Nothing like this existed in Boulder at the time. Maybe Boulder needed its own Beta?

In order to answer these questions, I began calling on my support network for advice and input. I explained the concept of SF Beta and solicited their opinion on how that model might fit within our existing ecosystem. Although many pointed out the challenges of introducing yet another event, they also acknowledged that our community wasn't perfect and that there's always room for more great things.

I arranged a meeting over coffee with a select number of the smartest Boulderites I knew to get feedback and shamelessly ask for sponsorship money. To my delight, I secured funding immediately thanks to a Googler named Alex, who worked at their local office. I then reached out to the founder and organizer of SF Beta, a complete stranger, and I sold him on the opportunity of expanding his model to our unique community. Within a few months of hustling, Boulder Beta was born.

In February 2011, we launched with our first event. We featured 10 local startups at a bar downtown. Four hundred people registered and over 300 walked through the door to meet the companies and mingle with their fellow community members.

As of June 2012, we've produced seven events and are on a quarterly schedule. Each event has attracted around 300 attendees and to date we've showcased over 60 startups. More than 15 community members have volunteered their time to make the events operate flawlessly. I've brought on an official partner as co-producer, who ran the most recent event in my absence, while I attended the launch of Sao Paulo Beta, founded by Pedro Sorrentino, who became familiar with the event as one of our selfless volunteers.

I attribute all of this success to the overwhelming support from the members of the Boulder startup community. With their initial help, I built the event. With their continued help, it lives on and will continue to do so indefinitely. This is just one example of what passionate, active, and collaborative people can achieve, when they're all in the same game for the same reasons.

—*Tim Falls, SendGrid, @timfalls*

After spending a summer as an associate at TechStars, Tim travels the world for SendGrid as "the community guy" and spreads a little bit of the Boulder magic wherever he goes.

BOULDER STARTUPDIGEST

Tom Markiewicz is another example of a newcomer to Boulder who was quickly welcomed into the community. Tom co-founded a company called StatsMix and went through TechStars Boulder in 2008. Following is his story of Boulder StartupDigest (http://startuprev.com/b2) along with some suggestions about how to have a great startup event.

I came to Boulder four years ago to be part of the TechStars Boulder 2010 class. I knew the best way to meet other entrepreneurs was to attend local events, but finding the best ones was a challenge. As an entrepreneur, time is my most precious resource.

Despite the fact that many events were promoted by or held at TechStars, it was difficult to find them without a central reference source. Not all organizers posted events on the same web sites, some were on various mailing lists, and others just randomly posted to Twitter.

Luckily, I stumbled on the StartupDigest, a free weekly e-mail in over 80 cities worldwide that highlights the best startup events for the upcoming week. Sites that aggregate listings are a nice start, but make it difficult to determine which events are the most useful. In the case of StartupDigest, each city's e-mail is curated by a local entrepreneur, which ensures someone with similar priorities scours all the events.

In Boulder, Andrew Hyde initially curated our StartupDigest. When I noticed the weekly e-mail stopped as he moved on to other projects, I reached out and volunteered to start writing the digest. Since I was already spending a lot of time doing this work anyway, I figured my efforts would be helpful to the rest of the community.

Now, after almost two years of writing the weekly e-mail, I've made some observations and learned a few lessons about startup events.

- *Have a topic*. Nothing is less interesting or engaging than an event with no agenda. Would you schedule a meeting with no plan? Of course not! Don't fall into the trap of creating a Meetup around a topic, but never specifying what is actually going to be discussed.
- *Good content matters*. Have a specific theme, speakers with interesting topics, product demos, or a panel of industry leaders. Should the content focus on programming, business, marketing, management, or customer support topics? In a nutshell, yes, all of the above work quite well. But the key consideration is what would someone working in a startup need or want to know about? Will attending this event enrich their startup life and help them move forward? If not, it probably doesn't constitute a good startup event. This doesn't mean the others aren't useful, but focus is important. And concentrating on the right events can definitely change a startup's trajectory.
- *Avoid the filler content*. What constitutes less useful content? If we define this as anything that doesn't give the entrepreneur the most benefit for the time commitment, then we have a whole host of criteria. These include happy hours,

general Meetups without topics, self-promotional sessions from vendors, and expensive courses masquerading as community events.

- *Vary the event's date and time.* For some reason, everyone wants to hold an event on Tuesday or Wednesday at 6 P.M. This must be written in the unofficial event planner manual somewhere. Each event is typically competing for the same attendees, and people, obviously, can't be in two places simultaneously. Furthermore, attending multiple events weekly in the early evening doesn't help with friends or family time, exercise, or any other extracurricular activities.
- *Schedule daytime events.* The lack of startup events during the day is surprising. Lunchtime is a great alternative, especially if you have a few good places to eat nearby. An example in Boulder is a monthly startup CEO luncheon. Each week there's a moderated group discussion focusing on a single topic, often accompanied by a sponsored lunch from a local law firm. It's an active and well-attended event.
- *Look beyond the local area.* Contrary to popular belief, locals will travel a bit further to interesting events. Once there's momentum and some success, local events can go beyond their immediate boundaries, as there may be new venues or interesting groups of people to reach. What works well for the local area will often be successful if expanded.

Each week I spend hours going through my resources, scanning all the available events, and communicating with organizers (who all think their event is the week's most important!) to discern the specific focus and scope of each event.

Despite the effort, the process provides its own rewards as it builds relationships and opportunities that would not be possible otherwise. Not only does it promote a vibrant quality to the community, but the digest has also become a focal point for new entrepreneurs to the Boulder area.

Its success is evident in our community. Readership of the Boulder StartupDigest has increased over 500 percent in the past two years, all of this without any outside promotional efforts, showing the service provides a valuable resource with its pointed recommendations and information.

—*Tom Markiewicz, StatsMix, @tmarkiewicz*

There is an important nuance in this story worth highlighting. Once again, our friend Andrew Hyde appears in the creation of another powerful resource for the Boulder startup community. Andrew is playing a non-zero-sum game at its finest: Rather than trying to hang on to each new thing he creates, he happily hands them off to others to run with them.

CU NEW VENTURE CHALLENGE

Many universities have some sort of business plan competition. In Chapter 9, I'll give you a deeper perspective on a different kind of university involvement in a startup community. For now, I'll give you a taste of the CU Boulder equivalent of a business plan competition. Brad Bernthal, a professor at CU Law, and one of the creators of the CU New Venture Challenge (http://startuprev.com/d4), describes it below.

If you cross a beauty pageant with a debate, plop it into a contrived startup competition format, and surround it with a revivalist atmosphere filled with entrepreneurial gospel, then you get the glorious mess known as the campus business-plan competition.

Such competitions are inevitably flawed. Time frames are artificial. Companies are at various stages of development. Hard emphasis on planning is at odds with lean startup practices. And only in the bizarre environs of a campus competition does a nonprofit seeking a sustainable way to fund an orphanage in Africa compete with a carbon-capture technology that would store greenhouse gases in the ocean.

Here is an even more curious thing. It somehow works.

CU Boulder launched its New Venture Challenge in 2008. We were not—and to this day are not—the first, best, or biggest competition. On the large side, Rice University is the gold standard of the campus business pageant world. Rice's competition is really an economic development event for Houston and its surrounding region. In 2012, the Rice competition featured $1.55 million in prizes and attracted entrepreneurs and investors from all over the world. Other competitions are more campus focused. The MIT $100K, for example, requires each team to have at least one team member currently registered at MIT. Business-plan competitions have proliferated across college campuses and, in all likelihood, your local university has one, too.

The story of the CU New Venture Challenge is especially interesting because we've stood up a viable, high-impact institution without a large gift or support from the main campus. It originated with an informal group of representatives from various centers—the business school, engineering, law, media and arts, the music school—involved in CU campus entrepreneurship. Paul Jerde of CU's Deming Center labeled us the "co-conspirators" and from the outset we were intentional about the goals for the competition. The co-conspirators decided that Boulder and the Front Range region of Colorado—including Denver, Fort Collins, and Colorado Springs—did not need a Rice-styled economic development event. Instead we sought to address student engagement in entrepreneurship.

Accordingly, the CU New Venture Challenge identified three objectives: (1) collapse the campus: convene cross-disciplinary congregations and stimulate interaction across departments; (2) create an entrepreneurial launch pad: provide a campus platform that answers the question, "Where do I start if I want to do a startup?"; and (3) provide a pipeline to the community: The CU New Venture Challenge should be a point of entry for CU students and faculty to get meaningfully involved in the region's startup scene. These three objectives drove the architecture of the CU New Venture Challenge.

First, in order to collapse the campus, the CU New Venture Challenge starts each year with kick-off events that are energetic, informative, and involve few barriers to entry. The goal is to have attendees from all parts of campus to get them interested in entrepreneurship. For content, events included a leading area entrepreneur's talk about how to pick a business idea worth pursuing, and a pitch night to facilitate team formation. To drive turnout, we assembled an executive committee of student ambassadors, with several students from each department on campus who served as evangelists to get the word out in classrooms and to relevant student groups.

In order to achieve the second objective—create an entrepreneurial launch pad to answer the question, "Where do I start?," we created a series of courses and modules. Credit goes to a business-school lecturer, Frank Moyes, who on a pro bono basis created a curriculum and taught a series of classes open to the public on a biweekly basis. Participants in the CU New Venture Challenge didn't have to attend these discussions, but this provided a platform for those who needed help. The classes were high impact for many students as well as for entrepreneurs in the community who attended these lectures. In recent years, we further tailored the courses to the subject matter of the companies and have introduced separate tracks for information technology, cleantech, music, and social entrepreneurship.

Finally, the CU New Venture Challenge created a community pipeline through a mentorship program. Each participating team is offered a mentor with relevant background in the team's area. Mentors agree to take at least two meetings with their assigned team. This allows great relationships to go forward by choice, but gives unproductive relationships a stop date. The program works because mentorship is more powerful in the context of a real problem as the mentor advises on the team's live issues. To date, the mentorship program has been a huge win as teams directly benefit from the mentor's advice and insights about their company. More broadly, the mentor interaction sets many participants on the path to full participation in the Boulder startup community.

A close friend frequently cautions not to let perfection be the enemy of the good. The glorious mess of the campus business plan competition, including the CU New Venture Challenge, illustrates this point. There is no way to get it right and satisfy everybody. Yet an offering that is experiential, hands-on, and catalytic for student involvement in startups is more than worth the cost of its imperfections.

—*Brad Bernthal, CU Law, @BradBernthal*

The CU New Venture Challenge will continue to evolve. However, one thing will stay constant: its inclusiveness across the CU Boulder campus and the broader startup community.

BOULDER STARTUP WEEK

Every startup community benefits from an events junkie. Andrew Hyde played this role for a number of years in Boulder and you can see his fingerprints on Ignite Boulder, Startup Weekend, and Boulder StartupDigest. Following is how Boulder Startup Week (http://startuprev.com/g3), another event Andrew co-founded, came into existence.

"You meet more people from Boulder at SXSW than you do in Boulder." It seemed like the third year in a row that we were having this discussion. The tech community of Boulder was doubling in size every year and I was somehow smack in the middle of it. "We need a big conference" was the sentiment everyone seemed to agree on. Putting on a weeklong conference was a costly endeavor and neither I nor anyone else seemed to want to leave what they were doing to put their full-time effort into such an event. Underlying this was fear that, even if someone put the effort into putting this together, no one would show up.

The best stuff at conferences happens in hallways and the after-parties, so I thought about simply structuring an event as a giant hallway. We could just create a free, decentralized event—no badges, no specific venue, and no checking in. The entire event would be one big hallway through the Boulder startup community.

I talked to a few friends and within an hour we had chosen the name Boulder Startup Week, purchased a domain, tossed up a simple web page, and set up a few free tools for RSVPing. I e-mailed 20 friends around the community to ask them to lead talks or activities in their offices or at a public coffeehouse. Within two weeks, we had 55 events planned over a five-day period.

Looking back on the first Boulder Startup Week I'm amazed it didn't fail horribly. The marketing plan was only for people to list their RSVPs through Twitter and Facebook. There was no money, no structure, and no organized leadership. There was no way to buy a ticket or contact anyone running the event with a question. We started planning just five weeks from the event date.

All we had was a startup community interested in interacting and sharing what they knew. The buzz built quickly. The community was saying, "Yes! We need this!," and almost every event was sold out weeks in advance. We kept adding additional events on a wide range of subjects and people started coming out of the woodwork to support the week, lead events, and offer to sponsor activities.

I didn't have a financial goal with Boulder Startup Week; I was doing it to help those looking to get involved in the community to meet others in the community. We raised enough sponsorship that we decide to fly people in from out of town to be part of a reverse recruiting event with Boulder startup companies. This had an extra benefit of getting the word out about the special things going on in Boulder, as many of the people from out of town blogged about the awesomeness of Boulder.

The week started with a bang—there were 11 events on day one. We had 11 other events each day for the full week. Each event was packed, and many of the public venues we had booked shut down their other business activities to accommodate the events. We had blogger, programmer, designer, marketer, and event organizer Meetups. The yoga session was a hit. The Ruby on Rails Meetup resulted in four job offers in one afternoon. The largest event was 1,350 people at Ignite Boulder; the smallest was 11 people who did the Easy Bike Tour of Boulder.

Of the 55 events, 40 had a focus on technology. The week flew by and we watched the community double as hundreds of new people, many living in Boulder, discovered an amazing set of people to spend time with.

I moved away from Boulder two years later to follow my dream of traveling around the world. The community picked up the slack and planned a second, then a third, Boulder Startup Week. Each year, the events get more interesting and the activity in the week grows; yet Boulder Startup Week continues to be a decentralized, chaotic volunteer event that pulls together the Boulder startup community for one week each year.

—Andrew Hyde, @andrewhyde

Boulder Startup Week just finished year three, and it was awesome. It's uniquely Boulder and a great opportunity for everyone in and interested in the Boulder startup community to engage deeply with each other for one week a year.

ENTREPRENEURS FOUNDATION OF COLORADO

When entrepreneurs are successful, they often want to give back to the community in some way. Ryan Martens, the co-founder of Rally Software, came up with a great model inspired by what he'd observed Marc Benioff do with the Salesforce.com Foundation.

When my previous startup, Avitek, was acquired in 1999, we missed a huge opportunity to talk about the role, benefit, and responsibility of leaders to make our community better as part of our commercial efforts. With our financial windfall, I turned to our local community foundation to figure out how to start making a difference locally.

I was shocked at the low level of philanthropy in our community, especially in contrast to the stark needs of many nonprofit organizations. From the perspective of the entrepreneur, the community really looked perfect. I assumed that you started philanthropy when you got older, upon retirement. I was naïve due to my laser focus on my business.

Brad Feld and his wife Amy Batchelor had the same realization several years earlier when I talked to him about it. He challenged me with the words, "If not us, who? If not now, when?"

I began an exploration to understand what other people around the United States were doing to bring corporate social responsibility into their startups. I noticed the great work the Marc Benioff (Salesforce.com CEO) and Suzanne DiBanca (Salesforce.com Foundation Executive Director) were doing. They had a model of 1/1/1 where they gave 1 percent of equity, 1 percent of time, and 1 percent of product to the Salesforce.com Foundation contribute back to their community in exchange for the support their community had given them in launching their company.

When we started Rally Software, we set aside 1 percent of our equity for the community. Although I tried, I was unable to get other companies and entrepreneurs to follow our lead. In 2006, Brad ran into Diane Solinger, the executive director of the Entrepreneurs Foundation in the Bay Area. Diane had figured out how to scale the model and encouraged us start an Entrepreneurs Foundation in Colorado. So in 2007, we adopted the Entrepreneurs

Foundation model and pulled together four other companies to act as founding companies.

The Entrepreneurs Foundation model is simple. With a volunteer board of local entrepreneurs, service providers, and local community foundation help, we make it easy for startup companies to endow the community. Typically, this means giving approximately 1 percent of a company's founding equity at a time when that equity is worth almost nothing. We've come up with a simple structure for this, which is a warrant for 1 percent of the company that is only exercisable upon change of control through a sale or an IPO. As part of the grant, the company decides how to allocate its equity into general community funds, specific community funds, or even specific charities.

With this simple step, the company signals a clear intention to do more for the community than simply provide jobs and create wealth for founders and employees. Although a company can simply join and make the grant, others engage in many other local philanthropic activities. The Entrepreneurs Foundation helps guide this, by providing education about opportunities, building skills-based volunteering efforts to develop leaders, and exploring strategic opportunities for the companies' products and services.

We treated this effort as a bootstrapped startup. We focused on finding the right people to get involved early while keeping expenses close to zero. We leveraged help from the Community Foundation Serving Boulder County, the other Entrepreneurs Foundation affiliates, and the Salesforce Foundation.

We started with a few board meetings, two recruiting events, and a few volunteering efforts each year. Over the first five years, we had several significant exits, a small portion of which was allocated to the Entrepreneurs Foundation of Colorado Operating fund, enabling us to hire an executive director. Several key local service providers, including KPMG, Trinet, Square 1 Bank, SVB, Cooley, and the Rocky Mountain Venture Capital Association, have helped us host and sponsor our events over the years.

Initially we added about 10 companies a year. With our increased resources, we now plan to add 30 companies a year. We have expanded our program to include a 1 percent of profit model for non-VC backed companies; our geography to include Fort Collins, Denver, and Colorado Springs; and our industries to include bio, cleantech, and LOHAS.

The power in the Entrepreneurs Foundation model is to connect startup efforts to the community right now, when it is easy. The result of this will be stronger communities, stronger businesses, stronger leaders, and more success at creating an entrepreneurial and empathetic society. That is the kind of place I want to live and work.

—Ryan Martens, Rally Software, @RallyOn

The activities and events listed here are by no means comprehensive. The Boulder startup community has a long list of additional activities, such as TEDx Boulder (http://startuprev.com/a0) started by Andrew Hyde), the Boulder Open Angel Forum (http://startuprev.com/d5) started by David Cohen and Jason Calacanis), the Boulder Jobs List (managed by me and David Cohen), and Startup Colorado (http://startuprev.com/m0) led by myself, Phil Weiser, and Jan Horsfall).

These activities are continually emerging and evolving. One particular one that has had incredible impact on Boulder is TechStars (http://startuprev.com/d6), a mentor-driven accelerator that was founded in 2006 by David Cohen. In the next chapter, we'll explore TechStars, its influence on Boulder, and the power of accelerators in general on a startup community.

CHAPTER EIGHT

THE POWER OF ACCELERATORS

On one of my random days in 2006, David Cohen came in and sat down. He introduced himself and slid a single sheet of paper across the desk to me, which had the outline for TechStars on it. As I read the document, David explained to me that he was an entrepreneur who had recently left the company that had bought his business. He'd made a few angel investments but wasn't happy with the dynamic of how the entrepreneurs engaged with him. He felt like his experience was wasted and there must be a better way for experienced entrepreneurs to help entrepreneurs who were getting their businesses up and running.

If these ideas, that of having entrepreneurs leading, having a long-term view, being inclusive, and engaging across the entire entrepreneurial stack, sound familiar, they should. TechStars uniquely hit on all four of the principles in the Boulder Thesis, and this is one of the reasons it is such a powerful construct.

I loved the idea and within 10 minutes told David I was in. He was raising $230,000 to run a single TechStars program, with $80,000 of the funding coming from him. I committed $50,000 on the spot and told him that I'd help him raise the rest. Following, in David's words, is how TechStars works.

In 2006, I realized that I wanted to make a living by doing what I love—investing in early-stage Internet software companies. Most angel investors lose money and I didn't want to be a statistic. By my calculations I was already at a disadvantage because I was based in Boulder, a small college town of only 100,000 people. In 2006, Boulder had some interesting things going on, but being a professional investor would almost by definition mean getting on airplanes regularly. I wanted to change that by importing talented founders, organizing and leveraging the community, and helping new startups here in very meaningful ways.

TechStars works by taking simple applications on the web; business plans are not accepted. We select and fund the best founders we can find who are working in interesting markets and put them together with the best mentors and investors for three months. The rest is pure magic. The model works only because we focus on the very best people, both as founders and as mentors. In our selection process, we have a very heavy focus on the team. In fact, we're fond of saying that the five things we look for in order are "Team, Team, Team, Market, Idea." Note that the idea is not the focus; it would be left off entirely if not for the dramatic effect of deliberately listing it last.

TechStars invests $118,000 in each of about 10 teams per year per location. Over 80 percent of our companies go on to raise venture capital or meaningful angel investment after TechStars. Most importantly, we've helped to create dozens of really fascinating and important companies, including SendGrid, Orbotix, and Occipital in Boulder.

I'm often asked why TechStars started in Boulder. My answer is always "because that's where I live and I love it here." Although

> TechStars started because I wanted to find a better way to make angel investments, the equally important reason was that I wanted to improve the startup community in Boulder.
>
> —*David Cohen, TechStars, @davidcohen*

David's vision for an accelerator had several unique components. First, it was mentor driven. His belief that entrepreneurs learned from other entrepreneurs, and that successful entrepreneurs like him wanted to give back by helping other entrepreneurs was at the core of TechStars from the very beginning. You should recognize the "give before you get" philosophy at work; mentors rarely knew what they were going to get out of TechStars but they engaged with the belief that it would be worth it.

Next, TechStars was both focused on and powered by the community and subsequently became a way to engage the entire entrepreneurial stack. The initial investors were local to Boulder as were most of the mentors. It was a 90-day program—long enough to be substantive, but not year round so no one got burned out. It was inclusive—while it was hard to get into TechStars as only a small percentage of applicants were admitted to the program, there were lots of community events, including the climax of the program (Demo Day).

Finally, David had a long-term view for TechStars. He knew he was going to stay in Boulder for the rest of his life, so he wanted to create something long-lasting that would have impact on the Boulder startup community for many years to come. Little did he realize when he started TechStars that he'd also have impact on a number of other startup communities.

THE SPREAD OF TECHSTARS
TO BOSTON AND SEATTLE

After the first year of TechStars, a number of entrepreneurs around the country reached out and asked if we'd bring TechStars to their city. Our mantra from the beginning was "quality over quantity," and although we had done a bunch of things right in year one, we decided to use exactly the same construct for year two. As a result, TechStars didn't expand beyond Boulder in its second year, although we helped other entrepreneurs get accelerators up and running by open sourcing and sharing the TechStars playbook.

After the second year we continued to be focused on quality and resisted the pull of an increasing number of entrepreneurs who wanted TechStars to come to their city. However, at some point, Bill Warner, a Boston-based entrepreneur who in 2008 had dedicated himself to reenergizing the Boston startup community, literally dragged us kicking and screaming to Boston.

Bill, who had previously founded Avid and Wildfile, two successful Boston-based companies, became exposed to TechStars when he met the founders from EventVue, a company in the first TechStars program. In 2008, Bill was working on the first MassTLC Innovation Unconference (http://startuprev.com/j2) and he wanted software to help manage it. This is what EventVue did and Bill ended up becoming an angel investor in the company. Shortly after, he came out to Boulder to see what was going on and learn more about TechStars.

He decided TechStars needed to be in Boston. He convinced us and we quickly recruited Shawn Broderick, another Boston entrepreneur to lead the program. Over a weekend we reached out to a number of Boston-based entrepreneurs, including Colin Angle (iRobot), Will Herman (Viewlogic), and Eran Egozy (Harmonix) to fund the first

TechStars Boston program. Within a month, applications were open and we were up and running.

TechStars spread to Seattle the same way. Greg Gottesman and his partners at the Seattle VC firm Madrona were considering creating an accelerator modeled after TechStars. They talked to Andy Sack, a successful Seattle entrepreneur, about leading the effort. Andy knew me well and wanted to simply do TechStars instead. He convinced Greg and his partners that we should bring TechStars to Seattle, and then they convinced David to expand to Seattle.

As TechStars expanded geographically, we continued to learn new things from each startup community. For example, Seattle pioneered the investment structure that we now use for all TechStars programs. Andy decided to be completely inclusive of the Seattle investment community and asked every Seattle-based VC and active angel investor he knew of if they wanted to participate in funding TechStars Seattle. With this approach, he was completely inclusive of the financing segment of the startup community. We didn't need the money for the program because we could have easily funded it with a small number of investors, but we wanted to be inclusive of anyone who wanted to engage.

TECHSTARS EXPANDS TO NEW YORK

TechStars now had a replicable model and accelerators were appearing around the world. We helped enable a lot of them by open sourcing the TechStars approach. However, we still knew there were other cities that we'd love to expand to. New York was one of these, and we were again fortunate to find someone to pull us to New York. This time it was David Tisch, a native New Yorker who was incredibly passionate about helping build the New York startup community. Following is David Tisch's story of how TechStars New York came together.

It was on or about August 25, 2010, when we sent out the first e-mail asking someone to be a mentor for TechStars NYC. This is the moment we started, the moment I knew this was real and there was no turning back. Within 48 hours, we had 40 of the top entrepreneurs in NYC on board to mentor companies we hadn't even found yet. We quickly raised four programs' worth of funding from 25 of NYC's best investors.

NYC's startup community is thriving right now, as has been well documented, and TechStars finds itself at the heart of it. Looking back, the establishment of TechStars in NYC has helped coalesce the startup community and is one of many factors at work.

Early on, I noticed that many of the mentors didn't know each other. This surprised me as I assumed that all the entrepreneurs in NYC working in and around the Internet would know each other. But that was wrong, and TechStars has become the place for mentors to meet each other and, more importantly, get a chance to work on something substantive—namely the creation of new companies—together.

The unique structure of our program brings together mentors (successful entrepreneurs, executives from big established companies, and top-tier investors), the TechStars companies (high-potential entrepreneurs working on big new visions), and top-tier investors from NYC. This trifecta creates a high-quality community with very little noise. The broader community rallies around the program on Demo Day, at the end, and the set of companies finishing the program that day.

In just under two years since we launched the program in NYC, TechStars has become a foundational component of the NYC startup community. The magic lies in building a community of deep engagement, where entrepreneurs can work shoulder to shoulder with other early-stage companies, building a support system that grows program to program.

—*David Tisch, TechStars NY, @davetisch*

Today, TechStars has geographically based programs in Boulder, Boston, Seattle, and New York. TechStars runs a vertically focused accelerator around cloud computing (TechStars Cloud) in San Antonio. It operates the Microsoft Accelerator (http://startuprev.com/n2), which currently has programs for startups building technology around Microsoft products, such as Kinect and Azure. It also co-founded the Global Accelerator Network (http://startuprev .com/f0), an organization for helping independently owned and operated accelerator programs. Although TechStars is six years old, it is still in its infancy, and its leaders continue to be committed to developing long-term startup communities in their cities.

ACCELERATORS ARE DIFFERENT THAN INCUBATORS

As the mentor-driven accelerator phenomenon has spread across the world, many organizations have started calling themselves accelerators even if they share few characteristics in common with TechStars. This is predictable, especially since we've been extremely open about everything related to TechStars, including our structure, how we operate, and our results.

However, one particular type of organization, the "business incubator," has recently started to be relabeled as an accelerator. Incubators have been around for a long time, with the first known incubator, the Batavia Industrial Center, having been created in 1959. Although incubators share some characteristics with accelerators, they are significantly different, and they play a different role than accelerators in the long-term health of a startup community.

Incubators were originally created to foster economic development. They provided entrepreneurs space, infrastructure, and advice in exchange for a fee, which was occasionally partially paid in equity. Incubators are typically nonprofit entities or attached to a university. Although some for-profit incubators have emerged, most are an extension of an existing investor's activity and are often linked to the Internet bubble.

Incubators operate year round and continuously. They focus on providing infrastructure and exist to fill up their space with paying customers. This often ends up creating a least common denominator effect rather than the highly competitive dynamic that occurs with accelerators.

Although incubators serve a useful purpose, and many have helped startups become successful, it's important to differentiate between accelerators and incubators. Each will continue to evolve to meet the needs of entrepreneurs and startup communities; I encourage those running incubators to celebrate their difference and focus on improving what they do, rather than trying to tie them more closely to accelerators.

UNIVERSITY ACCELERATORS

The constraints and resources of a university are unique and can play a powerful role in the startup community, which we will discuss in more depth in the next chapter. For now, let's explore how an accelerator could work in a university environment by taking a look at the program being created at MIT by Bill Aulet, the managing director of the Martin Trust Center for MIT Entrepreneurship.

For students interested in entrepreneurship, MIT functions as a ramp where students can build their entrepreneurial knowledge and skills so they reach escape velocity upon graduation. This approach ramp works well for many students, but some high-level students found it lacking, and eventually dropped out of MIT or openly considered dropping out to start a company instead of finish their college education. They pointed to Ellison, Jobs, Gates, and Zuckerberg. They heard the calls from Peter Thiel to drop out of college (http://startuprev.com/o2). They were fascinated with TechStars, Y Combinator, and similar programs.

As we tell entrepreneurs, when there is a crisis, there is great opportunity for innovation. So at MIT we took some of our own medicine and explored what we could do to meet this challenge of making the academic environment more conducive to successful entrepreneurial development.

We looked at Stanford, Berkeley, Harvard, the University of Michigan, and the University of Washington. We discussed the issue with students and saw their high level of interest in TechStars, Y Combinator, Dogpatch Labs, General Assembly, and Rock Health.

We recognized an opportunity to create a program unique to MIT's mission, using our assets, which would fit well with existing university-based and outside programs. MIT's mission is to educate our students and have a positive impact on the real world. We have a unique role in that we are an honest broker—a resource to all, beholden to no one. Our assets include an extensive value chain of innovative and entrepreneurial resources already in place, which we can easily leverage and expand to support a new program.

The program borrows heavily from the best practices of the outside organizations, but we did not simply copy their programs, because they already execute them well, and as a 501(c)(3) nonprofit we do not want to appear like a commercial entity, an accelerator of for-profit companies.

Our primary guiding principle behind the first summer MIT Founders' Skills Accelerator (http://startuprev.com/e0) is to help our students time compress the process of learning critical venture creation skills. We organized the accelerator around space, funding, structure, and status for our students.

Our research found that having a common work environment was extremely important for students, giving them a sense of community that results in their learning faster because they learn from each other, get emotional support to experiment, and are motivated by their peers.

The funding allows students to work full-time on their projects without worrying about paying their rent. Each MIT student receives $1,000 per month, and the team is eligible for up to $20,000 in no-strings-attached milestone payments if they meet agreed-upon goals in the areas of customer development, product, team, and finance. The payments are the incentives for students to buckle down and focus on learning entrepreneurship skills.

The structure is enough to keep the teams moving without inhibiting their flexibility and taking away their proactive muscles, as we did not want to create domesticated animals that cannot live outside the MIT bubble. The students have access to MIT's full mentoring network and we help them plug into that system based on their needs.

Twice a week the students get together and discuss what they've done, learned, plan to do, and need help with. We then provide a quick clinic on a topic relevant to their current state, ranging from how to build a persona to how to develop a founders' agreement.

Each team is assigned a committee, which serves the purpose of a temporary board of directors. All the members of the committees have substantial board experience and meet monthly with the teams. The committees also determine whether the teams get their milestone payments and at what levels.

Finally, the program provides students with the status of being part of an approved MIT program that makes it clear entrepreneurship is supported and legitimate. We find it particularly useful to assuage parents that no, their students are not slacking off playing video games all summer, but are doing a lot of work. As one student said, "Being selected is like getting a Rhodes scholarship in entrepreneurship."

—*Bill Aulet, MIT, @BillAulet*

In the six years since TechStars was founded, accelerators have quickly become a powerful part of a startup community. Although universities have had entrepreneurship programs for decades, many have grown stale over time and don't suit the needs of many of their students while providing relatively little value to the extended startup community. Bill Aulet's example of co-opting many of the concepts of an accelerator for the university environment is a powerful example of how a university can think differently about entrepreneurship. For more, let's now spend some time exploring how several leaders at CU Boulder have created a dramatically different example of university involvement in a startup community.

CHAPTER NINE

UNIVERSITY INVOLVEMENT

U niversities are a useful and important part of a startup community. They are feeders that, at a minimum, generate a steady stream of new young people into the startup community. However, there are many additional things a university can do to enhance the startup community.

When I tell people that the heartbeat of high-tech entrepreneurship at CU Boulder is the law school, the typical reaction is, "Huh?" CU Boulder is one of the strongest state schools in the United States, and it is the crown jewel of the CU system. How is it possible that the law school, instead of another location on the campus, is a focal point for entrepreneurial activity?

SILICON FLATIRONS

A dozen years ago, Phil Weiser, now the dean of the CU Law School, started an initiative that is now called the Silicon Flatirons Center. I tease Phil constantly about the name because I strongly believe "Silicon [Insert Geographic Landform here]" is not a good name for anything. He responds, as every dean should, that a significant financial contribution will cause a name change. Phil started Silicon Flatirons as a project in the law school around "international telecommunication policy and innovation." Over the years, it has become a key national convener of the various constituents around telecommunications, software, and Internet innovation. Several important concepts have emerged from Silicon Flatirons' discussions, including the idea of net neutrality.

In 2005, Phil and his colleague Brad Bernthal started focusing some of their energy on entrepreneurship. Phil and Brad realized that entrepreneurs drove innovation activity, especially around software and Internet. Given this, the policy discussion needed to include entrepreneurs, and Silicon Flatirons could be a great convening force for this.

Phil and Brad took it one important step further. Rather than trying to control the discussion, or create a dedicated entrepreneurship center at CU as a part of Silicon Flatirons, they simply turned things inside out. They put the word out to the Boulder startup community that Silicon Flatirons was a resource for them to use. They opened the doors to their building and offered it up as a regular meeting space for the startup community (the Boulder Denver New Tech Meetup happens monthly in "the courtroom," a large auditorium at CU Law). They expanded the law school's entrepreneurial law clinic to get the law students out into the startup community via free legal support. They reached out to partner with entrepreneurship-minded individuals across campus to start the New Venture Challenge, a campus-wide business-plan competition. They used the Silicon Flatirons platform to regularly bring amazing, interesting people to the CU campus to engage with the Boulder startup community.

They refused to play a zero-sum game. They worked hard to spread their entrepreneurial activities across the CU Boulder campus. With the ATLAS Center, Brad Bernthal and I started an Entrepreneurs Unplugged series, during which we interviewed a relatively unknown local entrepreneur each month, introducing them to CU and the local community. They spread the CU New

Venture Challenge across the campus, providing leadership but not taking ownership of it. They worked hard to do whatever they could to encourage other parts of CU Boulder to engage with the Boulder startup community.

In 2009, Phil went to Washington, DC for two years and worked in the Obama administration, spending the last year of his tenure as the head of innovation policy. During this period of time, he engaged deeply in a number of issues and initiatives around innovation and entrepreneurship. When he returned to CU as dean of the Law School in 2011 he was unambiguously focused on continuing to push the edge of entrepreneurship within an academic environment.

Following are some direct thoughts from Phil Weiser on how Silicon Flatirons impacts the Boulder Startup Community.

At the Silicon Flatirons Center for Law, Technology and Entrepreneurship, we have three core objectives: (1) to support entrepreneurship; (2) to prepare and encourage students at the University of Colorado to take advantage of opportunities in the tech sector; and (3) to raise the level of discourse on technology policy. In terms of achieving these objectives, there is nowhere better in the country for us to be than Boulder. A big part of that is the symbiotic relationship we enjoy with the vibrant and dynamic startup community in and around Boulder.

Our work in building Silicon Flatirons—and in providing a platform for Brad Bernthal to develop and drive our Entrepreneurial Initiative—led us to the direction of supporting entrepreneurship in the mid-2000s. In particular, Brad Bernthal joined us in 2005 with the aim of revitalizing our entrepreneurial law clinic, which serves community startups and enables our law students to gain unique legal experience. Around that time, we also started working closely with Brad Feld, who has sponsored our Roundtable Series on Entrepreneurship, Innovation, and Public Policy, which engages entrepreneurial leaders in policy discussions. When I returned as dean of Colorado Law in 2011 after working as the point person on innovation policy in the White House's National Economic Council, it was clear that our blossoming efforts to engage with and support the startup community—all under Brad Bernthal's leadership—were paying dividends to our students, faculty, and fundraising efforts.

Supporting entrepreneurship by serving as a convening platform and as an interface between the University of Colorado and the startup community is a core commitment from Silicon Flatirons to the community. From the beginning, we recognized that our affiliation with the University and an ability to be an honest broker—we are not trying to sell anything—is an asset that we can and should use to support the startup community. With our platform, we host the monthly Boulder Denver New Tech Meetup, the Entrepreneurs' Unplugged events (with national and local success stories ranging from Ted Turner to Charlie Ergen to Dan Caruso), and a regular crash course series (on topics from immigration issues to marketing to managing IP licenses). With respect to supporting and encouraging entrepreneurship more directly, we do so on campus by sponsoring a New Venture Challenge competition and statewide by supporting the Startup Colorado effort.

For students at the Law School and across campus, we are emphasizing a basic point: you are all entrepreneurs now. Whether or not they join a startup or a large company, the reality is that all students should think of themselves as entrepreneurs. Preparing students to be successful entrepreneurs and to join the tech sector involves both providing a valuable set of skills and sparking students' imagination about the opportunities they can find at tech companies—locally and nationally. For the local tech companies, this means that we need to develop relationships with them and create opportunities for them to get to know our students. We are constantly looking for ways, such as some of the programs mentioned above, to do just that.

One core challenge for federal, state, and local technology policy discussions is that the entrepreneurs—and the companies not even born yet—are not represented. Engaging entrepreneurs—and would-be entrepreneurs—in discussions around technology policy issues is a constant challenge. In short, entrepreneurs are often too busy to take the time to get up to speed on the details of spectrum policy, the arcana of patent law, the details of digital copyright discussions, or any other range of policy debates that will shape the future of innovation in the information industries. At Silicon Flatirons, we make a concerted effort to bring issues back to first principles and examine them with a wide range of thought leaders, bringing local entrepreneurs and venture capitalists into the discussion. By so doing, we believe, we can pave the way for better policymaking.

In general, our philosophy toward the startup community is to "feed the network." We are always looking for ways to give back and create opportunities, such as hosting a Startup Summer program as part of Startup Colorado. In every such case, we find ourselves being enriched from our engagement with the community. And immersing ourselves in the values of the startup community makes us better at everything we do at Silicon Flatirons and has a very prosperous effect on the entire Law School and our students. The CU Law School and Silicon Flatirons' unique connection to Boulder's amazing startup community underscores what a valuable relationship can be established between entrepreneurial leaders and an engaged university community.

—Phil Weiser, CU Law, @pweiser

125

SOME COMPONENTS OF CU BOULDER

Like most universities, CU has many different departments, each with their own politics, hierarchies, and financial pressures. Some of these engage with entrepreneurs; a few of them have deep entrepreneurial programs. There is a lot of structure around this activity with advisory boards, specific programs, and formal economic dynamics around entrepreneurship.

A classical component is the "entrepreneurship center." Like many universities, the entrepreneurship center is located in the business school; in CU's case it is called the Deming Center for Entrepreneurship. It has an advisory board, dedicated classes, and many specific courses and activities around it. The MBA students can be part of a student group called GEA (Graduate Entrepreneurs Association), which is affiliated with the Deming Center. Although it's a solid program, it's embedded within the business school, and at times it has been relatively isolated from the rest of campus and the rest of Boulder. This has changed in recent years, partly due to a spirit similar to Silicon Flatirons, which seeks to connect the various entrepreneurial activities across CU. Consistent with this, the Deming Center has recently led efforts, including a cross-campus entrepreneurship certificate and an engineering management and entrepreneurship certificate, to help make entrepreneurship classes increasingly available to non-business-school students. Although these offerings sounds like no-brainers, the way money flows across campus departments can be a challenge, and the increased opportunities for non-business students to complete entrepreneurship certificate programs is a healthy development. Providing avenues by which students in any discipline can get involved in entrepreneurship helps get fresh blood into the system, an important function of universities, which I elaborate later.

Another typical component is the technology transfer office (TTO). In CU's case, the TTO is a separate group that has its own board and a revenue agenda linked to patenting and protecting university-generated research and extracting licenses or equity from companies built around this research.

In some situations the TTO is helpful in generating new companies, but it is generally separate from the local startup community.

The engineering school, which historically has not been focused much on entrepreneurship, launched its own entrepreneurship program (called Eship) in 2008. The Eship initiative did not go according to plan. Its brief history, nonetheless, underscores why experimentation can be a valuable part of university entrepreneurship. By 2012, with the creation and growth of a broader cross-campus entrepreneurship certificate at CU Boulder, Eship decided not to duplicate efforts. It folded its certificate into the cross-campus entrepreneurship program. Yet engineering continues to teach certain entrepreneurship courses originally established through the Eship curriculum. And the experiment continues to stimulate interest in entrepreneurship among engineering students. In short, Eship took a path different than what the engineering school had in mind, but it still led to some promising avenues.

Universities, especially departments within universities, too often see entrepreneurship programs as a near-term cash solution in an era of declining state support and rising tuitions. This is generally a mistake. Instead, universities need to fundamentally see themselves as preparing students to be players in dynamic industries that require entrepreneurial skills. There is no better context for this than startups. If universities take a long-term view of this process, then students who receive great training and get involved in entrepreneurship during their time on campus will ultimately succeed, and a fair share of those individuals will come back and make healthy donations to say thank you to a campus that helped their success.

CHALLENGES TO ENTREPRENEURSHIP PROGRAMS AT UNIVERSITIES

Although there are many interesting things going on at CU Boulder around entrepreneurship, there are some challenges that generalize to any university environment. Brad Bernthal describes three key challenges: (1) entrepreneurial engagement is not rewarded within the faculty incentive structure, (2) lack of resources for entrepreneurial programs, and (3) cross-campus collaboration is not in the DNA of a university. Bernthal provides solutions to each of them in the following section:

In startup conversations there is powerful rhetorical appeal to make the local research university the next—and you can fill in the blank here—MIT, Stanford, or similar research institution closely tied to a thriving startup community. What this actually means is seldom well defined and often frustrating to anyone trying to accomplish the goal of integrating entrepreneurship more deeply into the university.

The blueprint for a leading entrepreneurial research university is to be three things: (1) a community catalyst: a nerve center where the startup community convenes and information spillovers occur; (2) a magnet, teacher, and pipeline for the next generation of entrepreneurial talent into the region; and (3) a source of insight, ranging from innovative ideas that can be commercialized, to broad and fundamental understandings about what makes startups as well as startup communities work.

Formidable barriers in academia, however, present challenges to this idealized vision of an entrepreneurial research university. At least three reasons help explain why top entrepreneurial universities are the exception, not the rule. We've encountered all three at CU Boulder and have applied the solutions I describe below as a way to address each of them.

Challenge 1: Entrepreneurial engagement is not rewarded within the faculty incentive structure. Scholarship and basic research are the university's coins of the realm. Commercialization and entrepreneurship are, at best, viewed as a nice version of faculty service. At worst, junior pretenure faculty commits career suicide by getting too involved in these "distractions."

The solution is to not try to slay the largest dragon. True believers around entrepreneurship in a university float a vision that startups will count toward faculty tenure, and a high percentage of professors will become entrepreneurs. In almost all cases, this is false and results in a quixotic quest to start with the hardest problems on a campus. Instead, the true believers should pursue winnable opportunities unlikely to encounter institutional resistance. For example, my passion over the past five years involves what amounts to a startup within CU Boulder, known as the Silicon Flatirons Center's Entrepreneurial Initiative. Universities are great, natural conveners with often excellent and sometimes underutilized facilities. Leveraging this, we launched a series of public events that connect and celebrate the startup community, with the ambition to connect the CU campus and the software/telecom/geek portions of the entrepreneurial ecosystem. In the past year, we helped provide 48 public-facing startup events with over 6,500 attendees. We created a nerve center of startup activity on campus that did not require approvals or funding from central campus, the CU Regents, or other administrative bodies. It just required a few committed individuals within the university to move it forward.

Challenge 2: We don't have the resources to do X. Resource challenges typically take the form of shortages in the number of professors to teach classes, money to fund initiatives, and facilities to house programs. This is especially true today, given dismal and declining public support for American research universities.

The solution is to co-opt your community's resources. The best course I've been associated with is Venture Capital, a class that I co-teach with Jason Mendelson from Foundry Group. Similar patterns of community involvement, such as hosting the Boulder Denver New Tech Meetup, reinforce our roles as conveners in the community. In a similar vein, CU's Entrepreneurial Law Clinic helps form and launch 20 startups a year, which is made possible by a network of 15 volunteer attorneys who work closely with law students to supervise the clinic's work. The town-gown combination of full-time professor and expert practitioner, which is powerful and underutilized within academia, enables a university's entrepreneurship efforts to take flight without having to be entirely self-funded and self-sufficient.

Challenge 3: Cross-campus collaboration is not in the DNA of the university. Entrepreneurship is a cross-functional activity and cuts across many departments in a university. Often each department that gets involved in entrepreneurship wants direct and immediate benefits from its efforts. Departments and centers each chase the same donors, are architected as individual silos, and lack a tradition of rewarding interdisciplinary work. Finally, members of different department efforts are regularly compared in a winner-take-all fashion.

The solution is to pick your rival intelligently. Focus the campus and supporters on the real competition, which is a competing university, not the department across the street. At CU Boulder, I highlight that the real competition is the University of Texas (and Austin), the University of Washington (and Seattle), Duke and the University of North Carolina (and Research Triangle Park), and leading universities in startup communities in India, China, Brazil, and elsewhere.

Furthermore, leaders on campus should identify common projects to work on that span the campus. This nurtures trust, opens lines of communication, and sends an important signal of collaboration to the community. For example, half a dozen organizations at CU Boulder jointly built and run a cross-campus entrepreneurship championship series, titled the CU New Venture Challenge. One of our objectives is to collapse the campus and assemble wide numbers of individuals that rarely connect in other contexts.

Campus efforts to catalyze entrepreneurship, like the startups they seek to promote, involve significant risk of failure. When they fail, this should be accepted and not punished. When they succeed, although there is rarely the equity upside for the campus participants that accompany startup success, the experience built in the context of the university is powerful. Connecting a university to a startup community prepares students to perform valuable roles in growing industries and, in turn, the community benefits from a university that provides talent, opens its doors, and fosters an environment that celebrates the startup.

—*Brad Bernthal, CU Law, @bradbernthal*

WHY THEY DON'T WORK IN ISOLATION

Like most universities, CU has many activities around entrepreneurship spread throughout the entire campus. In isolation, each is interesting and occasionally does something that is additive to the startup community. However, these activities are fragmented, often opaque to outsiders, and difficult to engage with. Furthermore, hierarchies tend to dominate; within each department the resources available, people involved, and academic structure tend to follow a classic hierarchy.

Because the Boulder startup community uses a strong network approach, the leaders tend to engage in places in which it's easy to engage. Silicon Flatirons created this type of environment and, as a result, many of the leaders in the Boulder startup community have engaged deeply with Silicon Flatirons and CU Law. If you did a survey of the 500 or so people at any random Boulder New Tech Meetup and asked if they had ever been to the Deming Center for Entrepreneurship, my guess is that fewer than 20 percent of the people in attendance would have been.

Fortunately, the leaders at CU, including Phil and Brad, are taking a long-term view. They recognize that the university is a feeder and needs to be a key resource for the startup community, rather than a leader. As a result, they've adopted a network view, both within the startup community, by opening their doors wide and being a convener for any activity that someone in the startup community wants to initiate. They've done the same across campus by being as inclusive as possible with courses, programs, and activities, in some cases against their direct financial interest in the context of the Byzantine university accounting approach.

This leadership has impact on other leaders at CU who, over time, have realized that a networked approach is much more powerful than a hierarchical approach. As a result, professors throughout the school who are interested in entrepreneurship are less concerned with how it impacts their department and, instead, simply are engaging in whatever is going on that is interesting to them.

THE REAL VALUE—FRESH BLOOD INTO THE SYSTEM

Universities provide one key input into the startup community—a steady stream of smart young people. Some of these students will be interested in being entrepreneurs; others will be interested in working for entrepreneurial companies. Either way, if the startup community can connect effectively to these students, it's a huge win for the university, the startup community, and the students.

I'm always fascinated by the reaction I get when I talk to students in entrepreneurship classes. Recently, I gave a lecture at an MIT class called Founders Journey. It was a Course 6 class (computer science) and the room was full; I was the guest lecturer near the end of the semester. During my class, I asked how many of the students intended to start a company right out of college. Only a few hands went up. Although I was surprised, I started asking random people in the room why they took the course. Almost all of them said that they wanted to learn what it was like to be an entrepreneur, better understand what it would be like to work in a startup, and have some context for the future when they might want to start their own company. I then asked them how many wanted to work for a startup, rather than a big company, after graduating. Almost every hand in the room went up.

There are many different ways to engage students with local startups. Ben Limmer created one approach, called startups2students, while he was a sophomore at CU Boulder when he grew worried that he was going to end up in the bowels of a mega-corporation doing something he hated. Following in Ben's words is how startups2students came about:

> Since I can remember, I told my family that I was going to work with computers and technology. After graduating high school, I went off to CU Boulder with a desire to learn more about the delightfully

geeky world of computer science. The first year of classes flew by. Then, sophomore year came around. The classes were still interesting, but I started thinking about my career opportunities after college. I knew there were lots of jobs available in my field of study, but I was worried that all the opportunities were at megacorporations where I would not be able to have a tangible impact on the company's success or failure. Panic set in. Maybe computer science wasn't the right direction for me.

After trying to hash things out on my own to no avail, I went to two of my professors whom I trusted, Clayton Lewis and Dirk Grunwald. Both Clayton and Dirk were surprised to hear that my biggest concern was working for corporate giants because they knew something I didn't. Unbeknownst to me, I was in the midst of one of the most thriving startup communities in the country. The fact that CU Boulder was so isolated from the surrounding startup community scared all of us. We set out to change that.

To help support this goal, Dirk suggested that I restart a group that had been defunct for some time, the Computer Science Undergraduate Advisory Committee (CSUAC). We reinstated the group with passionate undergraduate students who wanted to help mold the CU experience for other computer science students. We wanted to be a catalyst for change and infuse the Boulder startup community with the pool of talented students at CU.

After a few brainstorming meetings, CSUAC decided that the best way to kick off a new relationship between CU and startup companies was in one big bang. Why not host an on-campus event where local entrepreneurs could come in and talk about their companies? Maybe some students could get summer internships or even full-time positions from an event like this. Instead of overthinking it, we just went for it. If it flopped, at least there would be pizza.

CSUAC largely left the planning of the format of the event up to me. I wanted the event to be quick and fun, with the primary focus on networking between students and startup companies. I wanted to encourage a dialogue between students and entrepreneurs, instead of the usual "students as consumers"–style presentations I had been involved with in the past with corporate giants. Technology is something interesting and the opportunities are endless. I wanted to empower students to dive into the trenches with these technical visionaries and try to connect people with whom they shared common passions. Therefore, I limited company presentations to a maximum of three minutes to give the students a tiny glimmer of what each company sought to do and encourage them to learn more after the presentations via direct conversation.

We organized the event by leveraging every connection we had to the startup community. After seeding the discussion to several professors, I was connected with Brad Feld and David Cohen. After exchanging a few e-mails, both Brad and David were intensely excited to get me in touch with local startup companies looking for fresh talent. Suddenly, my inbox was inundated with e-mails from local entrepreneurs who were interested in meeting motivated CU students. We booked the tiny Computer Science Educational Lab and started signing up companies for the first startups2students event. Before I knew it, three months had passed and we had 13 companies and over 50 students confirmed to attend. We were going to need more pizza.

On the evening of the event, the room buzzed with an excitement I had never seen before among the students. Passionate students listened intently to the short presentations prepared by each of the companies, scribbling notes of people they wanted to approach. The presentations flew by, and when the networking time came around, commonly introverted computer science students were shaking hands and connecting with CEOs and CTOs of fascinating startup companies. The amount of excitement and passion in the room was dizzying. Toward the end of the event, I stood back and observed the room. I knew that CU and the Boulder startup scene had made the important initial connection that would last beyond my college experience.

For the last two years of my college experience I, along with help from CSUAC, meticulously grew the event each year with a bigger venue and more exciting new startup companies offering internships to students. The second year had 15 startups looking for interns and employees. The third year had 20. We had to start giving away "nonpresenting" spots to try to keep startups2students true to the original vision of short presentations with a focus on networking. After I graduated in 2011, I entrusted the event to the next generation of CSUACers. I was elated to be attending startups2students 2012, not as a student, but as a full-time employee of a company I was introduced to through startups2students.

Launching the startups2students event is something I will always be proud of. Not only did the event help me, personally, to discover my place in the technology world, but it also acted as a catalyst to get CU Boulder and the Boulder startup community connected. To this day, I love hearing from people that found their current job or internship through startups2students. I love that some of my former classmates went off and started their own startup companies. To anyone interested in starting an event like startups2students, go for it! It takes time and dedication, but it is incredibly worth the effort. Worst case, if it flops, at least there was pizza.

—*Ben Limmer, @l1m5*

Another approach, used by Bart Lorang, the CEO of FullContact, is to engage aggressively with the Colorado School of Mines Field Session program. Bart describes the program, the engagement with the students, and the results:

The founders of FullContact recently trekked to Colorado School of Mines (CSM) in Golden, Colorado, to attend one of my favorite events: Computer Science Field Session presentations. Not familiar with the School of Mines? You should be. It's a terrific engineering school; in 2011 it was ranked 29th in America among public universities.

Field Session is quickly becoming an annual ritual for us. We head over to School of Mines around 10:30 A.M., watch incredibly gifted computer science students give their presentations, cheer on the demos, share a few laughs, then afterwards we all head over to Woody's Wood-Fired Pizza for a celebratory feast.

Field Session is a capstone course that lets CSM computer science students apply everything they've learned to date by working for six weeks with an actual company. Students work in teams of two to four people and are expected to work 40 hours a week for the duration of the project. At the end, they should have analyzed a problem, produced a design, and implemented and documented a solution.

The CSM teams self-select the companies and projects they want to work with. Hoping to get that COBOL program converted into a Windows DLL? Good luck getting a team onboard. Only the coolest projects and best companies end up with a team.

The value proposition for both parties is simple. Students get real-world experience working inside a company with real deliverables and an opportunity to impress a prospective employer (not to mention course credit). Companies get an injection of young talent into their organization for a short period of time, a working deliverable, and the chance to evaluate potential hires.

In 2011, we were fortunate enough to score an amazing team of four CSM students. The start of the project happened to coincide with the beginning of TechStars Boulder. As a result, FullContact had eight people jammed into the TechStars bunker and our CSM team was forced to work out of the supercramped "pillbox" in the back. But they were good sports, and they got to witness some of the TechStars magic firsthand. They even attended Demo Day and watched us pitch. Our team turned out to be very bright and incredibly gifted, so much, in fact, that two of them have come aboard FullContact to work with us full time.

This year, we were able to land two incredible teams. Like last year, we made the conscious decision to treat CSM teams just like employees. Our feeling is that if we treat the CSM teams like interns, we'll get intern-like results (i.e., less than ideal). But if we treat the teams like full-fledged team members, they'll do better work and be more likely to want to be part of our company in the future.

As a result, we fully assimilated the CSM teams into our daily, weekly, and monthly processes. The teams worked from our office every day—this time in Downtown Denver—and took part in our daily stand-ups. They also took part in our weekly demos, retrospectives, one-on-ones, and monthly all-hands-on-deck meetings.

This year, we ended up with two awesome deliverables and four CSM students who have agreed to come aboard full time for the duration of the summer. Assuming all goes well, most of them will continue to be part of our team during the school year and beyond!

—*Bart Lorang, FullContact, @lorangb*

THE POWER OF ALUMNI

Internships and recruiting events are a powerful way to engage students with the startup community. Connecting the threads of the startup community with entrepreneurial alumni, especially those who have moved out of town after they graduated, is another powerful dynamic.

Although many universities look at their successful entrepreneurial alumni as sources of funding, I encourage them to make a huge mental shift and view them as leaders who can contribute back to the university in many nonfinancial ways. When they do this, they often get more money from the alumni than they would have otherwise, and they create a much more satisfying relationship with the alumni.

Almost all successful entrepreneurs who I've met have affinity for their school. You hear of stories about famous Stanford alums (Brin, Yang), MIT alums (Bose, Stata, D'Arbeloff, Swanson), and University of Michigan alums (Page, Costolo). Although you don't always hear about CU Boulder entrepreneurial alums, there are plenty of them, including Glenn Jones (Jones Intercable), Libby Cook (Wild Oats), Steve Ells (Chipotle), and other up-and-coming stars like Dave Morin (Path, Facebook) and Jeremy Bloom (Integrate).

There are a handful of very simple things universities can do to leverage the power of entrepreneurial alumni, especially those who have moved to a different part of the world:

Bring alumni back to campus: First, invite them back to campus annually and make it easy for them to come. Have them come on a Thursday where there is a lot of activity followed by a weekend sporting event. On Thursday and Friday, set up a series of student interactions, including a well-publicized seminar at which they talk about what they are doing, tour their department and the current research that is going on, attend a roundtable with a set of standout students working in the same area as the entrepreneur, and have lunch and dinner with interesting people. Make sure you know the social activities the alumni enjoyed and incorporate them into the mix. Make it friction-less—cover all travel and lodging, make it comfortable and easy. If they are sports fans, they'll stay over Friday night and enjoy a game on Saturday; if not, they can head home on Friday.

Create a mentor relationship with the alumni and a top student in his area. In Boulder, we've created a CU Alumni Entrepreneurship Mentoring program by which we match up successful entrepreneurial alumni with students who are interested in mentorship. This is a long-term, multiyear relationship during which no money changes hands, but the alumni agrees to be available on a regular basis with the student and meet face to face for a meal at least once a quarter. We've affiliated this with TechStars Boulder, so the alumni mentor and the student can easily engage in a part of the Boulder startup community by becoming part of the extended TechStars community and participating in aspects of TechStars during the summer if they'd like. Using a Facebook group, we've built a communication network across all the students so they can share their experiences with each other and build community among budding entrepreneurs at CU.

Highlight the alumni publicly. At CU Boulder I co-run a program called Entrepreneurs Unplugged. In this collaboration between Silicon Flatirons and CU ATLAS (Alliance for Technology, Learning, and Society), we do a Charlie Rose–style public interview with an entrepreneur on a monthly basis. Many of the entrepreneurs are alums of CU Boulder, and most of them are not high profile. This is an effective way to highlight them more clearly in the local ecosystem, especially around the university.

The relationship between a startup community and a university can be a powerful one, but it is often complicated. By focusing on specific activities and remembering that the university is a feeder to the startup community, great things can happen.

CHAPTER TEN

CONTRASTS BETWEEN ENTREPRENEURS AND GOVERNMENT

A reliance on government is one of the classic problems in startup communities that I discussed earlier. We routinely anthropomorphize government and say things like "Our government did X."

Although it's easy to fall into the trap of viewing government as an abstract entity, especially given the amount of time and energy it consumes around specific issues, it's important to always remember that government is a collection of people. Many of them are well intentioned, especially around anything that creates jobs or new tax revenue, but they often have no understanding of what entrepreneurs do or the pressures they face.

However, if you understand a few differences between entrepreneurs and government (and I recognize I'm anthropomorphizing in this case), entrepreneurial leaders can effectively incorporate government into a startup community. Let's go a little deeper on this topic and explore what government can do to be helpful.

SELF-AWARE VERSUS NOT SELF-AWARE

Great entrepreneurs are intensely self-aware. They know exactly what they are bad at and describe it often, as in, "This is what I suck at." Government leaders rarely talk this way. Entrepreneurs fail often and own it; government leaders rationalize why something didn't go their way. Entrepreneurs are directly critical of themselves and others and support their viewpoints with data. Government leaders work to "impact public opinion." It's a different vocabulary and a profoundly different behavior pattern.

In contrast, government leaders are chronically not self-aware. This is especially true in state and local governments, where the leadership often asserts that something is happening as though they wish it were. The assertions are often about activities in which the causality is completely misunderstood. This is often the case concerning economic development, which is the category that government puts a startup community in.

This is a problem only if the entrepreneurs rely on their state or local government to lead the startup community. Because many of the government leaders, and almost all of the government employees, have never been entrepreneurs, they can't relate to the dynamics of how entrepreneurship really works. Furthermore, although they can craft wide-ranging plans, do long-term studies, and create extensive white papers, they rarely can act quickly and precisely about a specific initiative.

BOTTOM UP VERSUS TOP DOWN

Entrepreneurs work bottom up and government works top down. When entrepreneurs start a company, they do all of the work. They don't have resources, staffs, structure, or a framework for what they are going to do. They just go do it. Government is exactly the opposite—there is a well-defined hierarchy, existing infrastructure, staff that persists from one administration to the next, and clear rules of engagement for getting things done.

Once again, we visit the theme of networks versus hierarchy. Entrepreneurs operate in a networked world; government operates in a hierarchical world. When these collide, it can be immensely frustrating to entrepreneurs as they watch government be ponderous, slow, and completely ineffective at handling issues that entrepreneurs could get done in a day. Entrepreneurs have little patience for this, especially when they see obvious decisions get tangled up in politics about other things that make no sense to entrepreneurs and have nothing to do with the issue at hand.

The solution for startup communities is to simply create a parallel universe of activity. Government is going to do whatever it is going to do around startups, entrepreneurship, and economic development. Some of this will be helpful; much will be a waste of energy. Entrepreneurs should engage in government-related things they believe will be valuable and that they find stimulating. However, they should not rely on any particular outcome from these activities or from the government in general. Instead, they need to create their own, durable set of activities for the startup community. Optimally, these activities will be bottom up and engage anyone in the community who is interested in participating.

MICRO VERSUS MACRO

Entrepreneurs often focus on the micro, that is, specific things that need to get done or will have impact. In contrast, government focuses on the macro. When I talk to leaders in government, they use words like global, macroeconomic, policy, innovation, and economic development. These are not words that entrepreneurs use; entrepreneurs talk about lean, startup, product, and people.

Several years ago I was giving a talk about the Boulder startup community to a cross-section of Boulder business and local government people. During the Q&A section, a woman I knew got up and said, "What do you think ecodevos should be doing to help?" I stood, stunned for a moment because I didn't know what ecodevos were. All I could think of was "Whip It" from the punk rock band Devo, and I had to restrain myself from blurting out "Whip It, Whip It Good." When I realized she was talking about her role, which was economic development for the city of Boulder, I said, "First, stop calling yourself an ecodevo since I'm certain there's not a single entrepreneur in the room who has any idea what that means." I then went on to make a few simple suggestions about how, as a feeder, the Boulder economic development people could be helpful, but the moment was defining for me since the language was so fundamentally different.

Every quarter I see reports in the local newspaper about things like increased/decreased amount of VC activity in the quarter, the number of patents granted as an indicator of innovation activity, and monthly changes in unemployment. Our governor makes an annual state of the state address in which he focuses on the changes in the state's economic output. The business newspapers report annual earnings, change in stock prices, and total compensation of executives in the same way they report box scores in the sports section. Almost all of this information is irrelevant to a set of entrepreneurial leaders on a long-term journey to create a sustainable startup community.

ACTION VERSUS POLICY

Entrepreneurs are hard wired to take action; government leaders focus on creating policy. Once again, there is a fundamental disconnect in language that can simultaneously consume an enormous amount of energy and make entrepreneurial leaders insanely frustrated.

I've been in numerous meetings with government leaders and their staffers talking about a particular issue relevant to entrepreneurship. In these meetings, I talk directly to the government leader, who engages charismatically and thoughtfully about the issue. Sometimes these conversations are robust and detailed; often they are 15-minute-long collections of talking points interspersed with niceties. After the government leader drops off the call or leaves the room, the real discussion with the staffers begin. Policy question after policy question gets asked. "How will this impact that?" "Why would this person over here, who clearly has a different agenda, support this?" "Could we add this language into what you are saying so there's a compromise?" "I'm not sure we can take this position because we need the support of so and so on something else."

In many cases, these conversations lead nowhere. In situations in which you have a strong, thoughtful leader like the current Colorado Senators Udall and Bennett, or a previously successful entrepreneur in Congress like Jared Polis, you end up with substance around entrepreneurship policy that can translate into action. Often, however, you just end up bogged down in the morass of additional policy talk in which no action can or will be taken.

This is especially true in state and local government. The length of time it takes to work through the policy discussion is often completely at odds with the urgency entrepreneurs feel. Recognizing the difference is sanity preserving for entrepreneurs and gives them a chance, should they decide to engage in the policy discussion, of actually having some impact. It is crucial to understand that this impact will only come over a long period of time.

IMPACT VERSUS CONTROL

Impact is a key word for all entrepreneurs. In a networked system, you want to have impact; in a hierarchy, such as government, you want to have control. Sure, many government people talk about their desire to have a positive impact, but they do this through having control. Entrepreneurs, on the other hand, are really only interested in impact and, if something doesn't matter, or doesn't work, they move on to the next thing.

It's impossible to control a startup community. This is the final, and possibly most important, reason government shouldn't play a leadership role. The natural tendency of government is always to control, that is, to set up hierarchy and bureaucracy that controls and sustains a particular structure. A startup community is a rapidly evolving, ever-changing thing. It doesn't need a long-term structure; that will emerge from the continually evolving activities of the entrepreneurial leaders. It doesn't need a hierarchy because it runs on a network model. Most importantly, it doesn't need any bureaucracy because this just slows down progress and the necessary and continual change that has to happen over a long period of time.

CHAPTER ELEVEN

THE POWER OF
THE COMMUNITY

Throughout the Boulder startup community we've developed a series of deeply held beliefs about how to behave and interact with each other. These beliefs evolved organically; there was no rules committee or hierarchy that voted on them. However, when you wander around Boulder, you'll often hear these phrases repeated or see these concepts in action. The ubiquity of them creates an amazing amount of community power.

GIVE BEFORE YOU GET

One of my deeply held beliefs to the secret of success in life is to give before you get. In this approach, I am always willing to try to be helpful to anyone, without having a clear expectation of what is in it for me. If, over time, the relationship is one way (e.g., I'm giving, but getting nothing) I'll often back off on my level of give because this belief doesn't underlie a fundamentally altruistic approach. However, by investing time and energy up front without a specifically defined outcome, I have found that, over time, the rewards that come back to me exceed my wildest expectations.

A group of us have worked very hard to incorporate this give-before-you-get philosophy into the Boulder startup community. You rarely hear the words, "What's in it for me?" around Boulder; rather, it's "How can I be helpful?" Introductions flow freely, as do invitations. As I travel around the country, I hear people talking about how easy it is to engage with people in Boulder and how good karma flows freely. This is give before you get hard at work.

A key attribute of a great mentor is someone who is willing to contribute time and energy to a mentee without a clear expectation of what is coming back. David Cohen talks about this constantly, and he leads by example, not just with TechStars companies but also with many other companies in which he's not an investor. TechStars has specific programs like TechStars for a Day (http://startuprev.com/n3) that are open to anyone who applies to TechStars, giving them a strong understanding of the mentor dynamics. And if you ask TechStars mentors why they participate, most of them say something like "Someone once helped me when I was a young entrepreneur; I want to give back."

There are definitely situations in which give before you get breaks down. When someone gets, and gets, and gets, and never gives anything back, it goes from tedious, to annoying, to uninteresting reasonably quickly. When a give-before-you-get philosophy is embedded in the startup community, people who only get but never give generate negative reputations and the startup community often rejects them, as a host organism rejects a parasite. So, make sure you are always giving at least as much as you are getting.

EVERYONE IS A MENTOR

The best moment in a mentor-mentee relationship is when the mentor learns as much, or more, from the mentee. If you ask most mentors why they do it, this is one of the core reasons. If you take a long view on the mentor relationship, it becomes clear that both the mentor and the mentee are actually mentors. If you extend this to the startup community, everyone becomes a mentor.

Often people ask me what they can do to help the Boulder startup community. One of my responses is to find one person they can mentor. Focus on your specific skill or background, and let the community know you are willing to mentor one person on this. Show up at the startup events, like the Boulder New Tech Meetup, and announce that you are an expert at thing X and you are willing to teach it to one other person. Better yet, hold a regular seminar, Meetup, or open office hours around it.

The culture of widely sharing knowledge, experience, and expertise is incredibly satisfying and self-reinforcing. The more you do, the more you'll see others in the community do. There are gems everywhere, often undiscovered, that appear when everyone becomes a mentor.

EMBRACE WEIRDNESS

Boulder is a weird place. In the 1960s when the hippies were driving to the Bay Area from the East Coast, some of them ran out of gas near Boulder. They looked around, liked the mountains, and decided to stay. Boulder's reputation of 25 square miles surrounded by reality is well earned.

In his book *The Rise of the Creative Class*, Richard Florida talks about weirdness as a key attribute of innovative communities. He's gone on to state, "You cannot get a technologically innovative place unless it's open to weirdness, eccentricity and difference" (*New York Times*, June 1, 2002).

The Boulder startup community embraces weirdness. You don't have to look a certain way, dress a certain way, or act a certain way. People can simply be themselves and are accepted for who they are and what they do. All you have to do is wander around for a few days up and down the Pearl Street Mall and you'll see what I mean.

BE OPEN TO ANY IDEA

I'll try anything once, as long as it's not illegal. I'm curious and I've found that the best way to learn things is to try things. Trying things and running experiments is a corollary to being open to any idea and has become well understood throughout the entrepreneurial ecosystem, especially in tech, as a methodology called the Lean Startup that has been popularized by Eric Ries.

In a hierarchy, when someone suggests something, the immediate reaction is to start asking questions and try to figure out why it won't work. In a network, the opposite approach often happens. When someone suggests something, just respond with, "Awesome—go do it." They either will or they won't. You'll recognize this as being similar to the approach of giving people assignments. You get a natural filtering process. If someone doesn't move forward with an idea, no time was wasted. If they do, then the results appear and often more people get involved.

Part of trying something is to understand how to fail fast. If you try something and it doesn't work, being able to either pivot based on the learning or call it quits and stop wasting time and energy on something that isn't working is key. However, if you don't try, you won't have the data to know whether something is working.

BE HONEST

A phrase my partners and I at Foundry Group have used for many years is "intellectual honesty." Our goal, simply stated, is to not bullshit one another. Regardless of the emotions you feel about a particular issue, decision, or situation, being intellectually honest trumps everything. Sometimes you have to dig deep to do this, especially when the discussion is heated or there are different opinions, but if you take an approach of always expressing yourself honestly and recognizing that you could be wrong, you put yourself in a much simpler and more powerful position in life.

This applies strongly to the dynamics of a startup community. There will be many different perspectives, motivations, opinions, and agendas swirling around. Individuals respond to feedback differently: Some need a lot of praise and are extrinsically motivated; others, like me, are deeply intrinsically motivated and although we hear praise, it doesn't really have much impact on us. Recognize that your startup community will cover a wide range of these behaviors.

Recently we held a Startup America Regional Summit in Boulder. In it, 120 people from 27 states descended on Boulder for two days to discuss how they were building startup communities throughout their states. This was the third Startup America Regional Summit as part of the Startup America Partnership (http://startuprev.com/n0) and it was an awesome experience. Afterwards, Christian Renaud, one of the principals behind Startup Iowa, wrote a really useful post titled What I learned in Boulder (http://startuprev .com/d7). In it, he captured nicely the concept of being honest.

> You don't get stronger and better by people telling you that you are already perfect. You get stronger by being pushed by your workout buddy calling you a big wimp and that you need to double your weight and double your reps or you're going to be the 98-pound weakling getting his/her butt kicked at the beach.
>
> This leads me to my second point, which is that . . . someone has to be the asshole. I was initially taken aback by the directness of the feedback that people were giving each other during the Summit as well as the Meetup. Brad Feld from TechStars in particular was direct, blunt, and challenging. After the initial shock had worn off, it

occurred to me that all of the feedback was constructive and probing, and not people trying to knock each other down a peg or two
because of their own low self-esteem. This requires that someone
needs to be the asshole in the room who doesn't keep the peace,
who challenges the quiet, who takes you on full-contact and makes
you stronger and better.

—*Christian Renaud, Present.io, @xianrenaud*

Although I don't encourage you to take on the persona of an asshole,
I think the idea of being direct, blunt, and challenging is a powerful one.
Plus, it's easier to always be honest because you never have to remember
what you said when whatever you said was the truth.

GO FOR A WALK

Too many meetings happen in conference rooms. There are great examples of
leaders who have meetings by going for walks. Steve Jobs immediately comes
to mind as an example. One of my most significant mentors, Len Fassler,
taught me this approach. Whenever Len and I had something serious to talk
about, we went for a walk. The numbers of times he poked his head into
wherever I was working and said, "Hey, Brad—let's go for a walk," are too
numerous to count. And, in the evening, after everything had settled down,
if we were together we'd often go for a walk and talk while he smoked a cigar.

I've adopted this approach and often walk when talking. I have a tread-
puter in my office (a treadmill from Steelcase with a computer on top) and
walk two to four hours a day when I'm in the office. When I'm on the road,
I'll often walk during my phone calls, especially in cities like New York where
I'd rather walk 30 minutes from one meeting to the next than hop in a cab.

I've adopted this in Boulder. Whenever I want to have a long discussion with a CEO or founder who I'm working with, or need to work through something with someone, we often walk out the door of my office and make a loop around town. More and more, I see other entrepreneurs walking and talking to each other, working through whatever is on their mind, while changing the context from a small conference room to the great outdoors.

Walking isn't the only thing to do. Seth Levine is a huge cyclist. He regularly hops on his bike and goes for a ride. In the book I wrote with David Cohen, called *Do More Faster: TechStars Lessons to Accelerate Your Startup*, Seth has a nice chapter in the Work-Life Balance section titled "Get Out From Behind Your Computer." In it, he describes how and why he bikes with entrepreneurs he works with.

My efforts at lunch rides and meetings started with Ari Newman, the co-founder and CEO of TechStars 2007 participant Filtrbox. The idea was purely social. Ari is an accomplished rider and we thought it would be fun to head out together for a ride. I quickly realized that to keep up with him on our rides, however, I needed to get him talking. So I started to ask him questions about his business, which was something I knew Ari, like all entrepreneurs, was happy to talk at length about. This was a natural extension of the more formal time we were spending together through the TechStars program, as I served as lead mentor to Filtrbox during their TechStars summer and continued working with the company after they exited the program and received institutional funding. Not only did these discussions have the desired effect of slowing Ari down, but our rides proved to be perfect settings to talk about the progress of the company. Away from the office, riding the hills of Boulder, it was easier for us to collectively gain perspective on the business that we weren't able to when we were physically confined by the walls of the Filtrbox office.

While my 2008 TechStars company was not as athletic and our meetings took place in the more typical format in a conference room, Ari and I continued to work on Filtrbox that summer on our regular rides. As I started mentoring Everlater in the TechStars program of 2009, cycling had become a meaningful part of my summer agenda. With a large group of cyclists involved in the Boulder tech scene, there were regular lunchtime rides throughout the summer (the group, called Geeks on Wheels, used Twitter to arrange rides). With this as the backdrop, it was natural to make cycling a central part of my work with Everlater's founders, Nate Abbott and Natty Zola. Nate, Natty, and I scheduled regular weekly rides (sometimes several times a week) and while we didn't keep a formal agenda, each ride had a number of topics planned out for us to cover. In this way, we worked through many of the early challenges the business faced as it moved from idea to reality in the course of the summer of 2009. Our typical rides lasted from 60 to 90 minutes, during which time we were able to focus on the business without interruption. And while getting some fresh air helps bring perspective, it's hard to avoid thinking about problems in a new way when you're out of the office, surrounded by the beauty of the Boulder foothills while your mind is completely clear.

It doesn't matter whether you are a walker, running, biker, or tennis player. Get out of your office and enjoy the place you live, while working with the people you are with.

—Seth Levine, Foundry Group, @sether

THE IMPORTANCE OF THE AFTER-PARTY

In many situations, the real party happens after the official party ends. This is strongly the case in a robust startup community, where there are many events happening all the time. Although some of these events have lots of room for socialization, especially at the grassroots level, others don't, or it's an awkward environment for this kind of interaction. This leads to the value of the after-party. Following are a few examples.

Each month, after the Boulder Denver New Tech Meetup, various groups informally descend on downtown Boulder. The event usually ends at 8, so by 8:30 there are clusters of folks having dinner throughout Boulder and they all know that if they want a final nightcap after dinner, the Bitter Bar is where they'll all meet up. According to Bruce Wyman, who was at many of the after-parties:

The Bitter Bar was easily the place with perfect after-party-like feel that catered to a deeply engaged crowd of geeks. The same care and passion that we brought in our respective fields and areas of expertise, they brought to drinks and cocktails. At the bar, there'd be a shared discourse on the bitters being made in-house that week or the sourcing of small batches of select bourbons while at the other end, it was easy to hear a deeply detailed discussion around the esoterica of load balancing and database duplication. The Bitter Bar provided the fuel and enthusiasm that propelled many people to meet, talk, and dream. Over time, people became well known and as you'd walk in, the mixologists would already be catering to your possible needs and meeting your new colleagues and friends. It was a family that kept growing and was equally as inviting as BDNT.

—*Bruce Wyman, @bwyman*

After every TechStars Demo Day there is always an after-party. Demo Day usually happens in the morning and finishes over lunch, but everyone is invited, including the broader community, to the after-party that happens in the evening. This is a final event of a TechStars class and is a chance for everyone to let off some steam while hanging out with all the people who have supported them.

Wherever Ben Huh, the CEO of Cheezburger goes, a game of Werewolf is sure to ensue. Ben travels constantly, evangelizing Cheezburger, and he often ends up deep in the mix of whatever is going on in a startup community that he's visiting. He loves playing Werewolf both as a way to get to know people better as well as to understand how they think.

Each of these approaches builds community. Your startup community might adopt some or all of these or create new ones of your own. Regardless, always remember that community is at the heart of a startup community.

CHAPTER TWELVE

BROADENING A SUCCESSFUL STARTUP COMMUNITY

hroughout this book, I've used Boulder as an example of a strong startup community. However, the Boulder startup community is still relatively young (only 40 years old with huge acceleration over the past decade) and has a number of weaknesses. In this chapter, we'll explore some of these weaknesses along with what some of the leaders in the Boulder startup community are doing to address them over the next 20 years.

PARALLEL UNIVERSES

Although Boulder has an incredible entrepreneurial density, it actually has five startup communities. I'm involved in the tech community, which I often refer to as software/Internet for clarity. The other four are biotech, cleantech, natural foods, and lifestyles of health and sustainability (LOHAS).

Let's focus on the natural-foods startup community. Celestial Seasonings, started in the 1960s, is one of Boulder's favorite natural foods companies, but did you know that two companies—Alfalfa's and Wild Oats—which make up about a third of Whole Foods, were started in Boulder? Or Izze? Or White Wave? Or Horizon Dairy? The list is long, and it keeps going since there is a robust contemporary natural-foods startup community spawning new companies every year like Justin's Nut Butter.

I'm a personal investor in Justin's, and I like Justin Gold a lot. I know Libby Cook, the founder of Wild Oats. I know Hass Hassan and Barney Feinblum, the founders of Alfalfa's and am an investor in their VC fund, Greenmont Capital, which is dedicated to investing in natural-foods companies. We are friends and say hello from across the room whenever we run into each other at a restaurant or an occasional event, usually of the entrepreneur-of-the-year variety.

However, the Boulder natural-foods startup community runs in a parallel universe to the Boulder tech startup community. To date, the intersection points have been weak and are artificial. The same can be said for biotech, cleantech, and LOHAS.

Recently, I was at an evening event organized by some of the leaders in the Boulder biotech startup community. They invited me as one of the leaders of the tech startup community as well as an investor, and a few other investors, to talk with some biotech leaders and entrepreneurs ostensibly about better linking the tech and biotech communities. When I got there, I realized I was the only person from the tech startup community. There were a handful of prepared remarks given in a casual setting. After 45 minutes of this, I realized the vast majority of these remarks were aimed at me, as an investor, and at the other investors in the room, to explain to us the amazing opportunities in investing in biotech. A core part of the argument was that returns over the past decade from biotech investing were better than tech investing; therefore, smart investors should invest in biotech.

At some point I was asked to give some comments. I started by saying, "You need to get rid of the chip on your shoulder about biotech." So much of the discussion was negative about tech in an effort to justify biotech investing. In my mind, this was classic zero-sum game behavior. I then went on to say that I thought the idea of creating linkages between tech and biotech was awesome, but they should be focused on community building across the entrepreneurs, not by getting tech VCs interested in investing in biotech. I also asserted that their macro data were irrelevant. Investors are not looking for the indexed returns of broad segments; they were looking to invest in extraordinary companies and get outsized returns because, if they didn't, they wouldn't be successful.

The event ended and I went on to dinner with a Boston entrepreneur who was in town for the upcoming Glue Conference (http://startuprev.com/c1). He's also a TechStars mentor and was spending time with the TechStars Boulder teams. As we sat down, one of the participants from the previous event walked in. He happened to be one of the successful entrepreneurs who had met with the Boston entrepreneur for dinner the previous night because they had overlapping interests in a company. We had a good chuckle about the small world of Boulder and a more serious exchange about how ineffective the previous meeting and discussion had been.

Several months later, there's been no follow-up, at least not with me. It's possible the biotech leaders in the room had enough of me, but my guess is their agenda, which was to try to highlight the biotech community to a few potential investors, was accomplished. In my opinion, this was a huge missed opportunity.

INTEGRATION WITH THE REST OF COLORADO

I-25 is a highway that runs from the top of Colorado to the bottom. There are four major cities located within a two-hour drive of each other. Fort Collins (population 150,000) starts at the top, then Boulder (population 100,000), then Denver (population 2,000,000), and, finally, Colorado Springs (population 750,000). Each city has a strong individual identity, and civic pride causes many to work hard to highlight their city as the best in the state. This results in another missed opportunity to connect the startup communities in an effort to amplify entrepreneurship across the state.

Although I spend plenty of time bouncing between Boulder and Denver, I spend very little time in Fort Collins or Colorado Springs. I've never invested in a company in either city and historically haven't felt particularly connected to either startup community.

A year ago I was invited to Colorado Springs to give a keynote speech at the Peak Venture Club about the Boulder startup community. Peak Ventures is the organized angel group in Colorado Springs. I said I was willing to come down, but let's make a 24-hour experience out of it. I offered to do a dinner the night before with the leaders of the Colorado Springs startup community, a talk in the morning, additional talks to students at University of Colorado–Colorado Springs during the day, and finish up with a lunch meeting with a group of young Colorado Springs entrepreneurs.

I drove down and settled into the beautiful Garden of the Gods hotel. John Street, an old friend and successful Colorado Springs entrepreneur (whose previous company MXLogic was based in Denver) picked me up and drove me to one of the most beautiful houses in Colorado Springs. There, overlooking the town, on a magnificent evening, I drank excellent wine, ate delicious food, and hung out with the patriarchs of the Colorado Springs startup community. "Old white guys" I thought to myself as we talked about what needed to happen to re-energize the Colorado Springs startup community. "We need more capital down here—there are no VCs." "We need better entrepreneurs." The conversation unfolded in a predictable way.

The next morning I attended a two-hour meeting of the Peak Venture Club. There were about 200 people in the room, many of whom were guests that day to hear my talk. Thirty minutes was consumed by announcements, followed by a few sponsors, followed by a few entrepreneurs presenting their companies. I then did my typical rant on startup communities and answered questions. After doing an interview with the local paper, I was shuttled off to UCCS where I gave a talk to freshmen in a seminar class about taking control of their future. I then ended up at a local gallery in Old Town Colorado Springs surrounded by 20 people under the age of 30. For the first time since I'd been in Colorado Springs, I saw diversity (race and gender), youth, and real startups. Almost every person in the room was starting a business except for the one person from the mayor's office. We had an awesome conversation. When they asked what they needed to do to get plugged into the patriarchs I met the night before, I said, "Ignore them. If and when you are successful, they will come to you. Go do something great and don't worry about them." Then I rode back to Boulder with my friend John, who had dinner with some entrepreneurs there that evening.

One of the people who attended the evening dinner overlooking Colorado Springs was Jan Horsfall. Jan is a successful entrepreneur who has been involved in several Boston-based companies but lives in Colorado Springs. He was at the Peak Ventures Meeting and sent me a note afterward that said essentially, "Okay, I'm in—time to bring some of the Boulder magic to this place." Since then, Jan has been working tirelessly to reenergize the Colorado Springs startup community using many of the things we've done in Boulder. In less than a year, the energy level in Colorado Springs is off the charts. Startups are coming out of the woodwork everywhere and the entrepreneurs are once again the leaders. The patriarchs didn't do it. The ones talking about it didn't do it. The government didn't do it. The entrepreneurs did it!

One of our year-one initiatives at Startup Colorado is to replicate the energy in Boulder in the other three front-range cities. Denver and Colorado Springs are off to great starts, with Fort Collins finally looking like it's kicking into gear. A year-two initiative will be to start more effectively integrating the activity up and down the Front Range. Check back in 20 years.

LACK OF DIVERSITY

Diversity in a startup community comes in two forms: ethnicity and gender. Although the population of Boulder is roughly split on gender, there's no denying the fact that the city is primarily Caucasian. Within the startup community, although it's getting better, there still is a meaningful imbalance among entrepreneurs between men and women.

Let's start with gender, because, in many ways, it's easier since the population is already roughly split between men and women. However, when you wander around the Boulder startup community, you see more men than women. This is especially true when you are in a room of founders.

Boulder is extremely inclusive, so it's nice to see the New Tech Meetups being 25+ percent women and an increasing number of women showing up at other startup events. Women like Krista Marks (Kerpoof co-founder/CEO), Nicole Glaros (TechStars Boulder managing director), Libby Cook (Wild Oats co-founder), and Nancy Pierce (Carrier Access co-founder) play active leadership roles in the startup community. However, we need to do more to include women in the Boulder startup community.

In 2005, I started working with Lucy Sanders, CEO of National Center for Women and Information Technology (NCWIT) (http://startuprev .com/a1). NCWIT has become the most knowledgeable organization about engaging women in computer science. Through activities like the NCWIT Entrepreneurial Alliance (http://startuprev.com/c2), NCWIT is working with entrepreneurial companies across the United States to engage deeper in getting more women involved in tech. As part of this, Lucy has some very specific ways for men to be advocates for technical women, as she's written about in her blog post, Top Ten Ways to Be a Male Advocate for Technical Women (http://startuprev.com/n4), which follows:

Following are 10 ways male advocates say they support technical women and promote diversity efforts in their organizations. These practices are derived from 45 in-depth interviews conducted by NCWIT researchers with male corporate employees in technology organizations or departments. Use these ideas to influence your own efforts.

1. **Listen to women's stories:** Male advocates in technical workplaces identify listening to their female colleagues' and bosses' stories about their experiences at work as one of the key drivers for their advocacy efforts. The women's stories alerted them to pressures and circumstances they might never have noticed. Let women know that you are interested in hearing their perspective if they are willing to share.

2. **Talk to other men:** Male supporters say talking to other men is critical. They raise awareness about why gender diversity is important, share what they have learned from women's stories, and intervene privately to correct discriminatory treatment, as needed. They suggest practicing what you might say in difficult conversations.

3. **Seek out ways to recruit women:** Because men outnumber women in tech, women must be actively recruited. Inviting female students to apply for internships, requiring hiring committees to interview a certain number of candidates from underrepresented groups, and providing promising minority employees with development experiences are just some of the ways men suggest shifting the status quo.

4. Increase the number and visibility of female leaders: Male advocates recognize that having role models for a diverse range of employees is important for recruitment, retention, employee satisfaction, and productivity. Raise the visibility of female employees and consciously develop more female leaders who can model a range of leadership styles. Provide technical and managerial opportunities, training, and promotions as part of this development.

5. Mentor and sponsor women: Although female role models are important, women actually benefit greatly from powerful male mentors. These mentoring relationships should be tailored to the individual's needs, but two common suggestions are helping women navigate "hidden rules" in the organization and making technical women's accomplishments more visible in the organization.

6. Notice and correct micro-inequities or instances of unconscious bias: Despite our best intentions, we are all subject to biases. When you see instances of unconscious (or conscious) bias in your organization, take action. Some suggestions include restructuring communication channels, moving people's desks or offices, paying attention to who speaks and who is interrupted in meetings, shifting departmental policies, adjusting salary discrepancies, or having one-on-one talks.

7. Establish accountability metrics: As the adage goes, what gets measured gets done. Effective male advocates describe establishing metrics to diversify internship programs, new employee interviews, hires, promotions, and even the makeup of project teams. When you make diversity part of what individuals are evaluated on in performance appraisals or for funding allocations, changes occur.

8. Model alternative work-life strategies: People in positions of power need to model work-life balance if these practices are to become respected and accepted. Setting aside time to attend family or personal events, publicly utilizing leave policies, and respectfully encouraging employees' alternative or flexible work hours are some ways men suggest doing this.

9. Make discussions of gender less risky: Sometimes it is easier for men to bring up gender issues because they are unlikely to be perceived as speaking in their own self-interest. Raise diversity topics in meetings; include information in newsletters or in professional development; and coordinate with female colleagues about how to best handle larger-group conversations.

10. Reach out to formal and informal women's groups: Male advocates stressed the importance of requesting invitations to technical women's meetings, participating in women-in-tech groups, and making sure that other men, especially top leadership, attend as well. Men also described the benefits of sending male colleagues to conferences like the Grace Hopper Celebration of Women in Computing.

—Lucy Sanders, NCWIT, @ncwit

In 20 years, when I look back, I expect that the gender ratio in the startup community leadership will be roughly equal, but it'll take another generation to get there.

Race is more difficult because there are so few minorities in Boulder. As a result, it takes real leadership, from people like Tom Chickoree (Filtrbox co-founder), who is leading a new TechStars program called RisingStars (http://startuprev.com/k0). This program extends technology-company startup opportunities to demographic groups that are currently under-represented in the tech startup community. It's a highly selective entrepreneurship-mentoring program, which pairs individual high-quality underrepresented entrepreneurs with individual TechStars alumni to help them develop the entrepreneur's vision into a viable company.

Although TechStars RisingStars isn't limited to activity in Boulder, Tom and TechStars are both based in Boulder, so it's a visible example of players in the Boulder startup community taking action along this dimension.

SPACE

Every rapidly growing startup struggles with space. When you are a company of three people, you can easily figure it out. A spare bedroom, coffee shops, co-working spaces, and the dark corner of a friend's office are all good places to start. By the time you get to 10 people, you are now paying a landlord rent. If you have rapid growth, you quickly run out of space, have to sublease your existing space (which can be even more complicated if you are already subleasing from someone), find new space, deal with the pain of moving, and then, when you outgrow that space in nine months, do it all over again.

This problem is exacerbated when you've got a bunch of rapidly growing companies in your city, especially if it's small city like Boulder. Everyone wants to be downtown because that's where the action and the entrepreneurial density are. However, growth in Boulder is deliberately constrained by the policies of the Boulder City Council, so there is very limited new office space. When existing inventory is tight, rents increase significantly. Being downtown becomes less cost-effective. Once you get over 100 people it is very difficult to find acceptable space.

It becomes an endless game of movable chairs that I've seen played out since the mid-1990s. It's particularly painful right now because there are numerous fast-growing companies that simply can't find space in Boulder. A year ago, people were still being creative about this. Recently they've given up and have started moving out to the edges of the city or to neighboring cities. In the short term, this creates space for new companies to fill but makes it harder to keep up the incredible entrepreneurial density dynamics of Boulder for the larger companies.

There are several initiatives under way in Boulder to address this. The first is a major new office development right in the heart of downtown where the old *Daily Camera* (our local newspaper) building sits. If done correctly, this could meaningfully expand the amount of available startup space in downtown Boulder. At the same time, several of the larger companies are looking to do a better job of linking up their expanding campuses with the downtown companies. Working in everyone's favor is the fact that the overall footprint of the city is relatively small—it's only a few miles from one end of Boulder to the other.

It's not clear to me that there's a solution for this other than focus on creating real startup neighborhoods within the community. In large cities like Boston this has resulted in a series of startup neighborhoods such as Kendall Square (Cambridge), Central Square (Cambridge), Harvard Square (Cambridge), Innovation District (Boston), Leather District (Boston), South End (Boston), and Rte. 128 (Waltham). The local entrepreneurial leaders work hard to connect these neighborhoods together in a larger startup community. I expect as the Boulder startup community continues to grow, we'll have to put more focus on this to sustain the incredible connectivity between people that entrepreneurial density drives.

CHAPTER THIRTEEN

MYTHS ABOUT STARTUP COMMUNITIES

'm not the only person who is spending a lot of time thinking about startup communities these days. The Kauffman Foundation has dedicated significant energy to this effort because they view entrepreneurship as the key to future economic vitality in our country and around the world.

As a result, I've asked Paul Kedrosky, a Senior Fellow at the Kauffman Foundation, to weigh in with some of the myths he regularly hears about startup communities. Although these myths are similar to some of the classical problems we discussed earlier, Paul brings a new perspective to the mix and hammers home a number of points made earlier.

We'll begin with one of my favorite myths: "We Need to Be Like Silicon Valley."

WE NEED TO BE LIKE SILICON VALLEY

It is usually among the first questions I get asked as I travel around the world researching and talking about entrepreneurship, innovation, and venture capital. The question is, of course, how can we create our own Silicon Valley?

To save time, here is the answer to the Silicon Valley question: You can't—you only think you want to.

Granted, everyone thinks they do. It has become a cliché, but there is a Silicon pretty much everywhere as you travel around, to the point that it is meaningless. It is also a reminder how many places get things confused, thinking that they can, by borrowing the trappings of the Bay area, create their own working facsimile of it.

The superficial trappings of Silicon Valley are obvious. They include: bountiful VC; research universities; lovely weather; a host of young technology startups; and a few large, successful companies. Further, weather aside, these trapping are surprisingly easily copied. You can attract VCs, especially if you offer state matching funds or subsidies; you can build or rebrand research universities; and you can start trumpeting various local startups and tech companies. This, of course, never works in the long term, as the discarded Silicon-everywhere names should tell you.

What is wrong with mimicking Silicon Valley in an effort to create your own? It is cargo-cult startup-community creation, not unlike the post–World War II stories of island cultures in the Pacific that created fake runways in hopes those air force aviators would return with money and trade. This blind mimicry of Silicon Valley confuses the resources of that particular community with the causes of startup community creation, growth, and renewal.

Much of what makes Silicon Valley or any startup community work has to do with things that happen below the surface. It has to do with the permeability of organizational boundaries, dictating whether people can move freely and bring their talents with them. It is driven by the continuous collision of young entrepreneurs in a dense urban environment who are coming, going, or simply milling about. It turns out that these successful centers see massive population turnover all the time, allowing the community to evolve, almost biologically. All of this is much easier to bring off in real communities than in giant entrepreneurial hubs that empty out on weekends like midcentury city downtowns full of skyscrapers.

There are deeper things going on. Much is made of the ease with which having failed entrepreneurially is accepted in Silicon Valley. This has many causes, including history and the U.S. genetic makeup, but it also has to do with simple geography: By being far from family and friends (California is a young state settled by immigrants), proto-entrepreneurs feel freer to try things than they would be if they were living across town from their family. A little alienation goes a long way in startup communities.

—*Paul Kedrosky, Kauffman Foundation, @pkedrosky*

Trying to create the next Silicon Valley is a fool's errand. If that's really your goal, save yourself a lot of heartache and simply move to Silicon Valley.

WE NEED MORE LOCAL VENTURE CAPITAL

Another common refrain that we touched on earlier is the notion that we need more local venture capital. Although there is always an imbalance between supply and demand of capital at any time in any market, Paul explains why equating startup communities and venture capital is a fundamental mistake.

I was in Brazil not long ago talking to some politicians about startup communities. Yes, they said, we are working hard on creating a more entrepreneurial city, so we have created a pool of capital to get more venture capital here. That's nice, I said, but let's get back to talking about startup communities. We went back and forth this way at least three or four times before it became clear they had made a false and common equivalency: Startup communities and venture capital are the same thing.

They were wrong, but they're not alone. Almost everywhere I go, people talk about venture capital and startup communities as if they are the same or, worse yet, that the former causes the latter. It is a lazy and convenient way of thinking and is a myth that inhibits a lot of progress, especially in nascent startup communities.

Venture capital is a service function, not materially different from accounting, law, or insurance. It is a type of organization that services existing businesses, not one that causes such companies to exist in the first place. While businesses need capital, it is not the capital that creates the business. Pretending otherwise is reversing the causality in a dangerous way.

Venture capital need not be located in your city for it to find opportunities to invest in. We operate in an increasingly flat and mobile world, one where investors quickly hear about interesting opportunities, no matter where they are located. They can find and even invest in deals online and from afar, through services like

Angellist (http://startuprev.com/b3) and Kickstarter (http://startup rev.com/e1). Even if venture capitalists miss a good deal, there is nothing like having missed one to convince investors to pay more attention in the future. Communities should spend more time showing investors what they've missed, and less time complaining that investors won't buy into promises of future gains.

Finally, venture capital simply isn't that important to startups. Less than one in five of the fastest-growing companies in the United States take any venture capital at any point in their history. Less than 0.5 percent of all new businesses in the United States ever raise venture capital. Where do they get capital if they don't get venture capital and they're too nascent for banks? The usual ways: friends, family, credit cards, and, the best way of financing a business—from their own customers.

Venture capital, while a wonderful accelerant of some companies, is neither necessary nor sufficient to create startup communities. While most entrepreneurs eventually need risk capital, it will come as a function of the opportunities presented, not before.

—*Paul Kedrosky, Kauffman Foundation, @pkedrosky*

ANGEL INVESTORS MUST BE ORGANIZED

The last myth we will explore is the idea that angel investors must be organized. There are examples of effective angel groups, but there are many more examples of ones that are merely a way for wealthy individuals to get together on a periodic basis and torture entrepreneurs. In the following section, Paul talks about the value of organized angel groups and why they are neither necessary nor sufficient for startup communities.

There is about a 50/50 chance that when I first meet a new angel investor in almost any city they will tell me a horror story about their local angel investing group. They may tell me about how they went to a couple of meetings, and stopped. Why? It takes too long, they'll say. These angels never write checks, they will complain. I can't take all the process, they'll say.

Most startup communities feel like they aren't complete until they have at least one angel investor group, one that meets regularly, screens companies, see pitches, and then, after group deliberation, invests individually in young companies. It is easy to see why they're so appealing as so much startup activity happens under the radar in coffee shops, garages, and online. Having an organized angel group that meets regularly and sees startups is an obvious sign that you are doing things to foment a startup community.

Great angel investing organizations exist all over the United States, and around the world, and they have invested in many great companies, as well as helping many angels become better investors. But like so much in a startup community, they are neither necessary nor sufficient.

For prospective angel investors who don't think they have enough deal flow or want someone to help them think through the screening or legal process, an angel investing group can be a good thing. But saying that some angel investors can benefit from being part of organizations doesn't mean that all will. Communities must feel that their startup community isn't working if groups of angel investors aren't meeting every Tuesday night in their city to screen startups.

Many angel investors are former entrepreneurs, with all that that implies. They are impatient, headstrong, and often fond of operating independently when they invest. Waiting for an angel group to come to a decision can be tough for such people, especially when you recognize that early-stage investing is intuitive, not empirical, and groups can tend toward a mean, shying away from risky and unusual investments.

The best startup communities embrace investing diversity. Some angels will want to invest through angel groups. They will find one another and form such groups. Other angel investors will operate independently. Neither approach is wrong, so startup communities should try hard not to fixate on angel groups and embrace both approaches.

—*Paul Kedrosky, Kauffman Foundation, @pkedrosky*

In Boulder, we've had several angel groups come and go over the years. Currently the two most effective ones are Open Angel Forum (http://startuprev.com/d5) and the Boulder Angels. Neither of these are formalized groups, but rather a loosely knit set of individual angel investors who periodically get together to look at promising companies.

John Ives, one of the members of the Boulder Angels, describes how it works.

Boulder is home to a small informal angel group, the Boulder Angels. The group was founded in January 2007 by eight investors who were increasingly unsatisfied with the existing, much larger and more organized angel groups in the Boulder-Denver area. The group found the large, formal angel organizations to be expensive and a poor source of deal flow.

Boulder Angels was created with two major assumptions in mind. First, we assumed an angel group could be very informal, lightweight, and nimble. We wanted to get moving and start helping the local startup community as fast as possible. We did not consider forming a corporate entity, hiring administrative help, or renting office space. Our group just started meeting for monthly lunches and began reviewing investment opportunities together.

Five years later, Boulder Angels has proven that angel networks can operate in an agile, informal manner. The logistics of running an informal angel group are minor. Boulder Angels administration requires minimal time to schedule monthly lunches and facilitate lunchtime discussions. Overall, coordinating Boulder Angels takes no more than three hours a month on organizational or overhead activities, two of which are at our monthly lunch.

Boulder Angels determined that it would rely on its own members to source and screen potential investments rather than a dedicated and compensated "deal screener." One of our unwritten rules suggests that members should perform sufficient due diligence before introducing an opportunity to the group, such that she is ready to commit to an investment. This does not mean that our members always fly solo. Quite often a subset of the group will coalesce to review and vet an opportunity.

What about all of the time invested in due diligence, leading a round, and supporting a startup over the life of the investment? All of these activities consume a significant amount of time. However, these activities are necessary regardless of the structure of the angel group. In other words, they are a fixed cost of startup investing no matter the structure.

A critical goal of any angel organization should be to build a network of trusted co-investors. The interpersonal relationships between angel investors are very important to the success of the group and the entrepreneurial teams. It is important to build a community of angel investors who share mutual trust and are comfortable being in the proverbial trenches with each other. In Boulder Angels, we believe that our strong personal relationships help us to move quickly when necessary and boldly when appropriate.

Boulder Angels has purposely grown slowly from 7 to 10 people over the course of the last five years. The slow, deliberate growth reflects another unwritten rule: New members are invited to join only after we have had good experiences co-investing with the new member. This is to ensure that we are adding people who are well-behaved investors and are well thought of by the Boulder startup community.

—*John Ives, Boulder Angels, @jives*

Although formalized angel groups can work, it is best to just get started developing strong interpersonal relationships based on trust, building your collective network in the startup community, and making investments in promising entrepreneurs.

CHAPTER FOURTEEN

GETTING STARTED

You can create a vibrant long-term startup community anywhere in the world. Throughout this book I've given you the Boulder Thesis, a framework, and examples. We've covered classical challenges and myths. As we wrap up, I want to leave you with a few examples from around the world.

GETTING STARTUP ICELAND STARTED

We will start with the story of Startup Iceland (http://startuprev.com/ i1). Although you may think of Iceland as a tiny rock in the middle of the ocean or the focal point of the global financial crises that started in 2008, today this country of 300,000 has a nascent but thriving startup community due to the efforts of a handful of entrepreneurs. One of them, who I've had the pleasure to get to know over the past year, is Bala Kamallakharan. Following is a description of how Bala helped get Startup Iceland started.

I always get crazy ideas when I have a lot of free time. The day was October 5, 2008, Sunday, and I was on a plane back to Iceland, where the government of Iceland had just announced that they would take over 75 percent of Glitnir, the third largest bank in Iceland. I was the newly appointed Head of India for Glitnir in Mumbai, and over the weekend I had been frantically trying to get hold of my boss, the CEO of the bank, or the CFO, or anyone who would pick up the phone and tell me what the hell was going on. No one did. That was the financial crisis that I saw from far, far away. The entire banking and financial system in Iceland had collapsed. I came back to Iceland and within a couple of weeks I was promptly fired from my job and the entire International division of the bank was shut down.

The country of Iceland revolted and the government of Iceland was brought down. There was an emergency government. I had a lot of time on my hands because there was not much happening and I started thinking, "What difference can I make?" Icelandic krona (ISK) had been devalued and lost 70 percent of its value, equity in most of the companies had been wiped out, national debt was through the roof, and everyone was talking about how spectacularly Iceland had sunk.

It was a tough time. I asked myself, "Where and how do we create value and equity?" I had an epiphany; the answer was entrepreneurs and startups.

I got to work and met every young entrepreneur and startup in Iceland. I catalogued all of them and saw that at the grassroots level there was a change happening that was not obvious on the surface. I made a personal mission statement that I wanted to help entrepreneurs and startups.

When I started on this I really thought the only thing the entrepreneurs and startups needed help in was in raising money. I was so wrong in that notion. I started reading everything that I could lay my hands on. I bumped into Fred Wilson's blog (http://startuprev.com/l4) and Brad Feld's blog (http://startuprev.com/o4 and http://startuprev.com/h1) and was amazed at the wealth of knowledge and wisdom that these two individuals were sharing freely on the Internet.

I met this small team sitting in the old fishing factory in the Reykjavik Harbor, working on text mining. They were each younger than 25 years old and called their company CLARA. They wanted to build a software-as-a-service company that helped gaming companies understand their communities.

I was startled. These kids were not worried about the ISK or the government or the global financial crisis or anything. They were building something and wanted to sell it to create value. I was impressed.

I found out that they needed capital to get their minimum viable product onto the market. There was a slight problem, as I had no money, so I reached out to my family and friends, convinced them to invest in Iceland and this young team called CLARA. My partners thought I was crazy but they indulged me. We invested in Iceland against all odds in 2009.

When all the other Icelandic entrepreneurs found out that I had invested in CLARA, I had a flood of requests to meet new companies. I took each and every meeting. It was painfully obvious to me that what the Icelandic entrepreneurial system needed was not just money but also mentoring and a bridge to a larger market.

I started doing research and found this thing called TechStars. I was blown away by the idea and started my campaign to move Iceland toward a startup culture, what I now call Startup Iceland.

Startup Iceland's mission is to build a sustainable startup ecosystem. One piece in that ecosystem is a mentorship-driven accelerator.

It took a lot of convincing to bring the two different incubators, a bank, and a bunch of mentors together. The result was Startup Reykjavik (http://startuprev.com/g4), an accelerator established in April 2012 that is part of the Global Accelerator Network.

The next piece in the puzzle was to build bridges to big markets. The only way that I thought we could achieve this in scale was to do an annual conference focused on entrepreneurship, making the participation and presenters really relevant so entrepreneurs around the world could come to Iceland and meet the local startups. Building bridges is about relationships and, in the hyperconnected world of Facebook, Twitter, Google+, one can connect online, but to really build relationships one has to break bread, shake hands, and look each other in the eyes. Conferences provide a fantastic platform for that.

I have never organized a global conference before; actually I have never organized any event that had more than 10 people. I just had this burning in the pit of my stomach that I had to do it. I slept very little, read everything, and lo and behold, Brad Feld wrote a blog post about startup communities. I wrote to him and invited him to come to Iceland. He did, we organized Startup Iceland, and the entire startup community understood what I was trying to do and rallied behind me.

We had our share of hiccups. The established companies, governmental agencies, and many people kept saying how this was never going to work, and some even thought it was the stupidest of ideas. I just shut my ears and kept at it.

The conference was hosted on May 30, 2012. We had a fantastic turnout with entrepreneurs traveling all the way from Singapore, South Africa, and Missouri.

Where do we go from here? There is a lot of work to do. A wise investor told me that the future is unpredictable, so he does not try to predict the future. We are starting to put the pieces in place for Iceland that increase the odds of success for startups and entrepreneurs. I believe it has to be done one piece at a time with a long-term view.

My dream is that 10 years from now people look back and say 2012 was a defining year in Iceland for startups, that Icelandic start-ups grow up to be global companies serving global customers in a sustainable way, and that entrepreneurs from around the world think of Iceland as a viable place to start their companies.

—*Bala Kamallakharan, GreenQloud, @balainiceland*

BIG OMAHA

Halfway around the world, Jeff Slobotski has been involved in creating a startup community in Omaha, Nebraska.

I started my journey into helping create the Omaha startup commu-nity about five years ago. I had always been fascinated and passion-ate around studying communities, whether within a social service or volunteer organization, political party, or the private sector. I've applied this energy to our startup community including the investors, mentors, university professors, and the entrepreneurs themselves.

I returned home to Omaha after working for a technology com-pany based in New York City. I had been exposed to the startup community that was developing rapidly in NYC along with those in San Francisco and Boston, and was fascinated by the level of con-nectivity and grassroots energy that was evident. When I returned home, I realized that we had the same quality of individuals here in Omaha and there was no reason we couldn't create a vibrant startup community here.

The entrepreneurs I met were heads-down and siloed, working on their own initiatives alone and largely unaware of what was going on around them. At the time, there was no outlet for telling the stories of the entrepreneurs working hard in our own backyard. This was the inspiration for Silicon Prairie News, a web site we started to highlight and document the individuals doing unique things in and around the greater Omaha, Des Moines, and Kansas City communities. Our goal has never been to build Omaha and the region into the next Silicon Valley; instead, we are focused on taking the strengths and assets that are unique to our region, and building upon them.

As we began connecting our startup community, we used online and offline methods. We held frequent local events for entrepreneurs including BarCamp, Startup Weekend, and other Meetups. In 2008, we hosted Sarah Lacy, a well-known technology writer (now CEO of PandoDaily) while she was on tour for her first book, *Once You're Lucky, Twice You're Good*. Over 150 people showed up for the event, and we were inspired to engage our community in the startup activity at a national level.

This motivation led to the creation of Big Omaha (http://startu-prev.com/h2). We had our first event in 2009 and this year we had 700 attendees from roughly 25 states and three countries. Through Big Omaha, we are able to connect the innovators and entrepreneurs within the region, but more importantly, presenters return to their cities outside of the region with a new sense of awareness about the Midwest. This builds bridges within the region, while connecting us with opportunities around the United States and the world.

—*Jeff Slobotski, Silicon Prarie, @slobotski*

STARTUP AMERICA PARTNERSHIP

The activities in Boulder, Iceland, and Omaha are now playing out regularly in cities through the United States and the world. In early 2011, in conjunction with an initiative from the White House called Startup America, a group of private individuals, foundations, and corporations launched the Startup America Partnership (http://startuprev.com/n0). I've been involved since the original inception of the idea in mid-2010 and today the Startup America Partnership incorporates many of the concepts of the Boulder Thesis and other ideas discussed in this book.

Shortly after it was created, Scott Case, the CEO, realized that a bottom-up approach was more powerful than a top-down approach. Donna Harris, the managing director of Startup Regions, Scott, and the team at the Startup America Partnership began an initiative to create a "Startup America Partnership" region in every state in the United States. Startup Colorado, which I co-chair, was one of the first regions to get created. Following, in Scott and Donna's words, are the attributes of a startup community they are actively driving to create in every major city and state in the United States.

America has historically been a natural athlete when it comes to startups—every city and state has a rich legacy of companies created by bold and ambitious founders who saw opportunities others didn't. Startups were the core driver to the cities' success and to our national strength. But today, natural athleticism is no longer enough—we live in a global economy, and our national success depends on our ability to focus energy on coaching our natural abilities to the next level.

The key to every successful startup community is startups. If you do nothing else, make sure all the founders and founding teams are visible and connected to each other. Beyond that, we've identified nine attributes of a successful startup community. No community is perfect on any of the measures. Where does your community stack up?

- *Leadership:* Strong group of entrepreneurs who are visible, accessible and committed to the region being a great place to start and grow a company.
- *Intermediaries:* Many well-respected mentors and advisors giving back across all stages, sectors, demographics, and geographies as well as a solid presence of effective, visible, well-integrated accelerators and incubators.
- *Network Density:* Deep, well-connected community of start-ups and entrepreneurs along with engaged and visible investors, advisors, mentors, and supporters. Optimally, these people and organizations cut across sectors, demographics, and culture engagement. Everyone must be willing to give back to his community.
- *Government:* Strong government support for and understanding of significance of startups to economic growth. Additionally supportive policies should be in place covering economic development, tax, and investment vehicles.
- *Talent:* Broad, deep talent pool for all level of employees in all sectors and areas of expertise. Universities are an excellent resource for startup talent and should be well connected to community.
- *Support Services:* Professional services (legal, accounting, real estate, insurance, consulting) are integrated, accessible, effective, and appropriately priced.

- *Engagement:* Large numbers of events for entrepreneurs and community to connect, with highly visible and authentic participants. The events include Meetups, pitch days, conferences, happy hours, startup weekends, boot camps, hackathons, celebrations, and competitions.
- *Companies:* Large companies that are the anchor of a city should create specific departments and programs to encourage cooperation with high-growth startups.
- *Capital:* Strong, dense, and supportive community of VCs, angels, seed investors, and other forms of financing should be available, visible, and accessible across sectors, demographics, and geography.

—*Scott Case, Donna Harris, Startup America Partnership,*
@tscottcase, @dharrisindc

You should recognize these concepts as appearing often throughout this book. Scott and Donna recognize that a big part of the value of the Startup America Partnership is consolidating the best thinking about startup communities and evangelizing them throughout the country to any city or region that wants to create a long-term startup community. It's been an honor to work with them as I honed the Boulder Thesis, testing it with them many times in different places.

DO OR DO NOT, THERE IS NO TRY

My favorite thing about startups is that they don't require anyone's permission. Great entrepreneurs just start doing things. These are the same entrepreneurs who can be the leaders of their startup community. They just do things, like many of the people you've read about in this book.

Although it's a long, challenging journey to create and maintain a startup community, no permission is needed. Startup communities exist all over the United States and the world. Some are already vibrant and durable; others are nascent. Hopefully this book has given you lots of ideas and inspiration to help take your startup community to the next level. Remember, it's a long-term journey, so be patient and persistent.

As Yoda once told Luke, "Do or do not, there is no try."

ABOUT THE AUTHOR

Brad Feld has been an early-stage investor and entrepreneur since 1987. Prior to co-founding Foundry Group, he co-founded Mobius Venture Capital and, prior to that, founded Intensity Ventures, a company that helped launch and operate software companies. Previously, Brad was an executive at AmeriData Technologies after it acquired Feld Technologies, a firm he co-founded in 1987 that specialized in custom software applications. Brad is also a co-founder of TechStars.

Brad currently serves on the board of directors of BigDoor, Cheezburger, Fitbit, Gnip, MakerBot, MobileDay, Modular Robotics, Oblong, Orbotix, SEOMoz, Standing Cloud, and Yesware for Foundry Group.

In addition to his investing efforts, Brad has been active with several nonprofit organizations and currently is chair of the National Center for Women and Information Technology, cochair of Startup Colorado, and on the boards of Startup Weekend and the Application Developers Alliance.

Brad is a nationally recognized speaker on the topics of venture capital investing and entrepreneurship. He writes the widely read blogs Feld Thoughts and Ask the VC. He has written three previous books: *Do More Faster: TechStars Lessons to Accelerate Your Startup, Venture Deals: Be Smarter*

Than Your Lawyer and Venture Capitalist, and *Burning Entrepreneur: How to Launch, Fund, and Set Your Start-Up On Fire!*

Brad holds Bachelor of Science and Master of Science degrees in Management Science from the Massachusetts Institute of Technology. Brad is also an avid art collector and long-distance runner. He has completed 22 marathons as part of his mission to run a marathon in each of the 50 states.

INDEX

STARTUP LIFE: SURVIVING AND THRIVING IN A RELATIONSHIP WITH AN ENTREPRENEUR

by Brad Feld and Amy Batchelor (2013)

FRIDAY NIGHT FIGHTS

A key to effective communication is to choose a time and place to talk when both partners are rested, ready, and relaxed, and to do this on a regular basis. If one or the other of you is exhausted or still wound up from the workday or processing some other emotional event, it will be much more difficult to have genuine connection.

When we were first living together and working at the same startup company, Friday night would often be the first time we had been together all week because of Brad's frequent out-of-town travel. Amy would want to have some connection and talk about our relationship, while Brad was just exhausted and didn't want to talk at all. Although neither of us is quick to anger, these conversations would almost always deteriorate into bickering and frustration, which didn't help either of us feel good. We often had social commitments of some sort—dinner, movie, friends—and Brad was often late or distracted from the week and still in the process of shifting gears. Amy was also often tired from her workweek and low on reserves of patience.

It took us an inordinately long time to figure out that we weren't fighting about our relationship, but we were merely tired and the end of a long week is just not a good time for intense communication. It sounds so simple now, but at the time it often felt like a weekly crisis. We changed the underlying pattern to dinner and a movie with only minor chitchat and no probing relationship queries from Amy until later in the weekend when we were both rested and ready. By doing this, we stopped having Friday night fights.

It's easier to defer needing to communicate to a better time if trust is developed that there *will* be a time for talking, and soon; the important business of communication will not always get moved down the priority to-do list behind other urgent (but not important) items. We did commit to catching up about what was going on in our lives every weekend—having this consistent weekly commitment was the basis for us being able to defer going deep on things on Friday nights.

Following is an example of how Friday night fights start from Brad's point of view. This happened recently, which is a good reminder that you have to keep practicing these techniques over time and that some of the underlying issues never really go away.

Friday night, at 6:20 p.m., Amy called me. My first thought was "F@#$—I screwed up." I answered the phone as I was walking down the stairs to the front door of my office building.

Me: "Hey there."

Amy: "I hope you are almost to Keystone."

Me: "Er, um, I'm just leaving my office now."

Silence.

I expect you've had a conversation that started that way and you know where this is going. Earlier in the day I had told Amy that I thought I'd be in Keystone, which is 90 minutes from my office, around 6:30, and suggested that we do dinner and a movie. Unless I had magically invented a teleportation device, I was going to be about 90 minutes late.

I apologized. Amy appropriately was pissed off. She expressed her frustration. I apologized again. Then she dropped the bomb—she was dressed up and ready to go out to dinner and see a movie that I had promised her earlier that day. Date night ruined.

I apologized again, told her I knew I'd blown it, and got in my car and headed to Keystone. I'd had a long, intense week (like most of my weeks) and felt crappy and demoralized. What I hoped was going to be a great, relaxing weekend with my favorite person in the world had started off completely wrong, entirely due to me not prioritizing us.

Twenty years ago, Brad bought a statue of Abe Lincoln, the Lincoln Memorial version, and put it in the middle of a bookshelf in our shared apartment. We were in our mid-20s at the time and we committed to "let Abe moderate our Friday night fights." Since he was a speechless inanimate object, his actual utility was to remind us of civil wars and great peacemaking. We quickly agreed not to have high expectations for our Friday nights as communication time. Instead, we would use them as a chance to wind down from the week, reconnect, and get aligned for a nice weekend together.

Here's how the recent developing Friday night fight described earlier was avoided.

About an hour into my drive, Amy called. She apologized for being so upset earlier. She was happy and cheerful, told me she couldn't wait to see me, and was just disappointed that my work had overrun my good intentions. I apologized again, but felt deep relief since I knew that we were back to a good place. I'd still screwed up, but at least we'd now have a chance to get things started on the right foot.

When I arrived in Keystone, I consciously made sure that I didn't rush to check my e-mail. We said hello, I played with the dogs as they greeted me, and then we made two cups of tea and sat down on the couch together. We spent the next hour catching up with each other on the week, just talking about what we had done and what we were thinking, all the while playing with our dogs. By about 9:30 we decided to call it a night. While not dinner and a movie, we started the weekend off right.

We still have our statue of Abe Lincoln. The tactic of waiting for a good time for real talking has served us well for many years.

Stay in touch!

Subscribe to our free Finance and Accounting eNewsletters at
www.wiley.com/enewsletters

Visit our blog: **www.capitalexchangeblog.com**

Follow us on Twitter
@wiley_finance

"Like" us on Facebook
www.facebook.com/wileyglobalfinance

Find us on LinkedIn
Wiley Global Finance Group